Palgrave Critical University Studies

Series Editor
John Smyth
University of Huddersfield
Huddersfield, UK

"This is quite simply a brilliant book, offering a critical analysis of impact and REF which is long overdue. Thomas focuses on the rise of the impact agenda in tourism and related subjects, but this book has a great deal to tell us about the nature of the neoliberal university, regardless of discipline. It is a must-read for anyone seeking to understand how and why the growing need to show a particular kind of impact from research is restructuring academia; this new agenda has far reaching consequences for critical researchers, so-called marginal subjects and for everyday working cultures in academic departments."

—Professor Rosaleen Duffy, *University of Sheffield, UK*

"This book presents a much needed, hard hitting and honest critique of the UK government's research impact agenda... Professor Thomas argues, rather controversially, but yet very convincingly, that tourism and related research has very limited impact due partly to the marginal nature of this sector in public policy terms.... the book goes beyond critique to present plausible solutions on how higher education institutions can and should generate impact. In this book Professor Thomas demonstrates that he is able to deal with serious and contentious issues in a very accessible, engaging and sometimes humorous way. This book is essential reading for all those who are concerned about the future of tourism higher education and who will be inspired to advocate for change in their own institutions, not just in the UK but across the world."

—Professor Donna Chambers, *University of Sunderland, UK*

"This is a novel exploration of the concepts and boundaries of the assessment of research impact as operating particularly in the UK. Its strengths lie in its personal perspectives and in the fact that it unpicks the policies and myths surrounding the impact process."

—Professor Gareth Shaw, *University of Exeter, UK*

Aims of the Palgrave Critical University Studies Series

Universities everywhere are experiencing unprecedented changes and most of the changes being inflicted upon universities are being imposed by political and policy elites without any debate or discussion, and little understanding of what is being lost, jettisoned, damaged or destroyed. The over-arching intent of this series is to foster, encourage, and publish scholarship relating to academia that is troubled by the direction of these reforms occurring around the world. The series provides a much-needed forum for the intensive and extensive discussion of the consequences of ill-conceived and inappropriate university reforms and will do this with particular emphasis on those perspectives and groups whose views have hitherto been ignored, disparaged or silenced. The series explores these changes across a number of domains including: the deleterious effects on academic work, the impact on student learning, the distortion of academic leadership and institutional politics, and the perversion of institutional politics. Above all, the series encourages critically informed debate, where this is being expunged or closed down in universities.

More information about this series at
http://www.palgrave.com/gp/series/14707

"Rhodri Thomas has delivered the perfect answer to the question: 'Does academic research have anything to say to understanding the nuts and bolts of tourism?' Witty, trenchant, clear eyed and level headed, it is an essential contribution...."
—Professor Chris Rojek, *City University of London, UK*

"In this timely contribution, Rhodri Thomas translates a perspective from within his disciplinary field of tourism, to portray the political antagonisms and inherent tensions that the modern, interplaying relational dynamics of research contest. The book pivots on the marketisation of Higher Education, and the subsequent neoliberal degradation of academic practice, and thereafter offers a nuanced and compelling account of the discursive representations of research impact, from the perspectives of various institutional bodies and actors, and their attempts to construct mythical value from research. The book deals not only with myth making around research value, but also critically evaluates the misconceived nature and actuality of research impact. Ultimately, the book re-evaluates impact, and returns to a traditional beneficiary of academic value from research and purpose for teaching, the student. The book therefore becomes an important source of knowledge, for academics across all critical schools of thought."
—Dr. Mark Egan, *University of York, UK*

Rhodri Thomas

Questioning the Assessment of Research Impact

Illusions, Myths and Marginal Sectors

Rhodri Thomas
School of Events, Tourism and
  Hospitality Management
Leeds Beckett University
Leeds, UK

PLYMOUTH UNIVERSITY

9 0096288854

Palgrave Critical University Studies
ISBN 978-3-319-95722-7   ISBN 978-3-319-95723-4   (eBook)
https://doi.org/10.1007/978-3-319-95723-4

Library of Congress Control Number: 2018948175

This Palgrave Pivot imprint is published by the registered company Springer Nature
Switzerland AG
The registered company address is: Gewerbestrasse 11, 6330 Cham, Switzerland

PREFACE

I started writing this book shortly after accepting an invitation to speak at the annual conference of the International Congress and Convention Association (ICCA) in Buenos Aires, Argentina. I was delighted to have been asked because it suggested that my work was meaningful beyond the confines of peer-reviewed publications and classrooms.

My presentation to ICCA delegates related to absorptive capacity, arguably one of the most influential ideas to emerge from management schools over the past twenty years. ICCA were road testing a new session format entitled 'the fast show', which required speakers to be succinct; as advised, I spoke for 90 seconds (i.e. 4667 miles travelled per minute speaking time).

During his allotted slot, a fellow speaker from the commercial world declared that innovation was merely about finding that 'wow factor'. As I thought about the simplicity of his declaration—but to be fair, he only had 90 seconds too—it raised questions in my mind about the occupational worlds we occupied and how knowledge claims were made and received in these environments.

On my journey home, I reflected further on the work of academics and their relationships with commercial practitioners, public policy-makers and those working in Non-governmental Organisations (NGOs). Developing closer affiliations with these constituencies, whereby academic research influences their practices, represents one of the corner stones of contemporary research policy in the UK and in many other developed economies. Increasingly, the expectation is that academics undertake research with (non-academic) impact as a condition of funding. As the journey progressed, I tried to piece together parts of a jigsaw which encompassed the aspirations of those responsible for research policy, the strength of the theoretical and empirical foundations on which research policy was built, and the behaviour of practitioners and academics. The structure for what I considered to be an interesting book began to crystallise.

The timing of this volume is also related to my completion of a series of impact evaluation and impact consultancy studies for the Economic and Social Research Council (ESRC) conducted with Professor David Parsons and, latterly, with Dr. Neil Ormerod and others. These usually involved examining the influence <u>on practitioners</u> of research undertaken by disciplinary (economics), interdisciplinary (sustainability) and multidisciplinary (social) research centres that represented 'major investments' for the Council, i.e. they had received substantial grants (multi-million pounds) to support their research and knowledge exchange activities. Following these, we undertook three projects which explored how social science research might be 'valued' and whether intermediaries might play a meaningful role in enabling impact. Although only passing reference is made to these studies, the process of undertaking the work has undoubtedly contributed to my thinking and helped shape the thesis advanced in this book.

Most of the literature that emphasises the potential contribution universities might make to innovation and national competitiveness is modelled on knowledge intensive, high value-added sectors of the economy, rather than those that are the subject of my research (tourism and related sectors such as events and festivals). Until now, there has been little systematic consideration of how contrasting sectorial dynamics influence university–practitioner relations. I offer a remedy by reviewing existing literature, reporting original research and providing ethnographic reflections on *pro-bono* and paid work undertaken with several professional associations and other agencies over recent decades. The latter relied, in part, on ESRC grant funding (RES-186-27-0015) and follow-on funding (RES-189-25-0205), both of which necessitated writing a persuasive impact plan and, subsequently, an account of impact. To an extent, this book also represents my 'sense making' of significant periods of working closely with practitioners.

My use of the term 'marginal' when referring to major sectors of the global economy may surprise many readers. Although economically significant, tourism is often *politically* marginal; in spite of their best efforts, industry representatives and lobbyists in the UK have failed consistently to impose their will on policy-makers. This is broadly representative of most complex modern developed economies. 'Marginal' also refers to the academic community involved in researching consumer, business and policy activity associated with tourism. With few exceptions internationally, departments that specialise in this field are not located in research-intensive (prestigious or highly ranked) universities. This sits in sharp contrast with other new 'vocational' fields such as city and regional planning or business and management studies. This matters because it influences the extent to which related subject associations are able to help shape the research policy agenda and how it is implemented. These fields are, in effect, marginalised.

The book is written for several audiences. Firstly, it is intended to inform those engaged in academic debates on research policy, impact and the role of academics in supporting innovation. It is also aimed at those whose research and scholarship encompasses knowledge flows, innovation and public policy development. I am hoping that those responsible for research policy will take note of the analysis because it demonstrates the need for a more differentiated approach than currently obtains. Finally, the book is written for academics in leadership positions within universities. By explaining why, on the whole, research impact is illusory for marginal fields and marginal sectors, more fruitful debates might be had about the potential ways of enhancing knowledge flows arising from the work of academic researchers. Perhaps the most obvious, but also most important, proposition advanced is the need to refocus on the role of academics as educators. This implies promoting good teaching that is scholarly and research informed to a variety of constituencies. I anticipate that this message will be dismissed by some, the predictable fate of those operating at the margins, but I hope it will be welcomed by many more.

Leeds, UK   Rhodri Thomas

ACKNOWLEDGEMENTS

I am pleased to acknowledge several organisations for funding research that has helped shape this book: the Economic and Social Research Council (ESRC) (grant references: RES-186-27-0015 and RES-189-25-0205), the Institute of Travel and Tourism (ITT), and the International Congress and Convention Association (ICCA). The remainder was paid for directly or indirectly by my employer, Leeds Beckett University.

A cluster of very recent past and current Ph.D. students is acknowledged because their overlapping interests helped me hone the position I adopt in Chapter 2: Dr. Yi Fu, Dr. Yanning Li, Conor McTiernan, Dr. Jackie Mulligan and Alistair Palferman. Some of the publications used to develop my argument in Chapters 2 and 3 would not have been written without the technical (statistical) contribution of two co-authors, namely Dr. Neil Ormerod and Professor Emma Wood. These acknowledgements do not imply that any of the above agree with my analysis.

Several senior practitioners have, over the years, agreed to participate in various innovative university–industry collaborations. I have learned much from working with the following: Steven Freudmann, CEO and Chair of the David Andrews, formerly CEO of Yorkshire Tourist Board (YTB) (now a part-time doctoral student), Joanna Royle, formerly Director of Marketing YTB, Jennifer Jenkins, Caroline Windsor, Nicole Leida, past Chairs of the Association of British Professional Conference Organisers (ABPCO) and Heather Lishman, its Director. Martin Sirk, until recently CEO of the International Congress and Convention Association (ICCA) and Alain Dupeyras, Head of Tourism at OECD, have also afforded me opportunities to collaborate and, by so doing, to gain the perspectives of thoughtful practitioners and policy-makers.

In relation to this book, I probably owe the greatest debt of gratitude to Professor David Parsons and Dr. Huw Thomas. Both have partici-pated at length in conversations on impact, engagement and the point of academic work in tourism and related fields. I suspect that one of them will agree in broad terms while the other will disagree with much of what I have written!

Finally, I am fortunate to work with many talented individuals both within and outside my own institution. I am indebted to them for their inspiration, tutelage and collaboration more generally.

CONTENTS

LIST OF FIGURES

LIST OF TABLES

CHAPTER 1

Setting the Scene: Markets, Competition and Research Impact at the Margins

If you had asked me 10 years ago, I would have said no,
but increasingly I do think it matters.
I do think we need to have more impact.
Research professor interviewed for this book

Abstract This chapter introduces the increasingly pervasive notion of research impact, i.e. the influence of academic research on non-academic constituencies. It positions research impact within wider discourses of neoliberal higher education policy and practice. It suggests that research policy and studies of impact do not differentiate sufficiently between disciplines or areas of socio-economic activity, both of which potentially influence the non-academic impact of research. The chapter argues for greater scrutiny of the dynamics of research impact within what are presented as marginal fields of enquiry and marginal sectors of the economy. It concludes by outlining the structure of the book and its thesis.

Keywords Neoliberalism · Universities · Research assessment
Tourism studies

© The Author(s) 2018
R. Thomas, *Questioning the Assessment of Research
Impact*, Palgrave Critical University Studies,
https://doi.org/10.1007/978-3-319-95723-4_1

INTRODUCTION

Much is made, particularly by academics, of the contribution academic research makes to innovation and the quality of organisational decision-making in the private and public sectors. The intensity of such self-justification has been fuelled in the UK by what is often termed the 'impact agenda'; public agencies funding research now expect researchers to demonstrate their worth by showing how their work has improved the lives or practices of others. For research councils considering funding proposals, this involves evaluating the proposed 'pathways to impact' or the actions to be taken to maximise the effect of grant funding on non-academic audiences (http://www.rcuk.ac.uk/innovation/impacts/) as well as the novelty, significance and sophistication of the planned research itself. For national audits of research quality, such as the Research Excellence Framework (REF) in the UK, evaluation is via impact case studies (www.ref.ac.uk/). Such concerns are not, however, confined to that country (see, for example, Fraser and Taylor 2016; Hicks 2012). Indeed, the importance of impact is such that the Australian government declared in 2015 that it was considering removing the evaluation of staff research publications as a means of allocating research grants and, instead, using measures related to impact and engagement (Watts 2017: 16).

Subject associations whose mission is to promote the interests of academics in their discipline or field now routinely profess the practical value of their members' academic work (see, for example: Academy of Social Sciences (https://acss.org.uk/publication-category/making-the-case/); The Chartered Association of Business Schools (CABS) 2015; Gerrard 2015). Publishers have also sought simple metrics for demonstrating impact in response to the changing sands of research policy. Perhaps the most prominent system to have emerged thus far is 'altmetrics' which combines the number of actors who have mentioned the research with the media used to calculate an 'attention' score (http://www.altmetric.com/publishers.php).

The rise of performance-based university research funding systems internationally and associated concerns with 'impact' has consequences for university research managers and for academic researchers. For the former, the status of their institution has become connected with their ability to perform well in research evaluation exercises. As result, universities that operate within such systems engage in strategic management (or game playing) to maximise their 'performance' and position in global league tables (Yudkevich et al. 2016). For the latter, promotion prospects are becoming influenced not only by an individual's ability to publish and to attract research grants but also by their capacity to generate impact (Bastow et al. 2014).

Although some researchers create arbitrary subject-based rankings (e.g. Park et al. 2011; Severt et al. 2009), performance-based research funding systems tend not to differentiate their approach to evaluation between disciplines or fields of enquiry (Hicks 2012). This is, perhaps, unsatisfactory when considering non-academic impact because there is evidence of significant variation between disciplines (Bastow et al. 2014). Moreover, while much energy has been expended studying the non-academic impact of universities with contrasting missions (e.g. Hewitt-Dundas 2012) and their relations with knowledge-intensive industries (e.g. Banal-Estanol et al. 2015; Bozeman et al. 2013, 2015), fewer researchers have examined non-knowledge-intensive sectors with the same degree of rigour (Thomas and Ormerod 2017).

The premise of this book is that greater scrutiny of the dynamics of research impact in different contexts is required. It is underpinned by a concern that is recognised by many but articulated by too few; a fear that academic researchers are becoming too embroiled in public relations strategies about their work (Marchant 2017) at the expense of their independence and criticality (Watermeyer 2016). It takes the form of an examination of tourism and related research which is argued to be a marginal interdisciplinary field of academic enquiry often related to a marginal sector of the economy, at least politically. Although the empirical work presented in this book is confined largely to the UK, the implications of the analysis presented extend to other countries operating performance-based systems, notably Australia, New Zealand, and (several countries within) the European Union.

INFLUENCING OTHERS AS A RESEARCH POLICY GOAL

There is a substantial normative literature that promotes engagement and influence. This often reflects the value systems of the academics concerned; those interested in promoting sustainability or corporate social responsibility, for example, are centrally concerned with finding ways of influencing individual, institutional or business practices for what they argue is the common good (e.g. Bramwell et al. 2016). Identifying behavioural or technical mechanisms for improving the sustainability of food systems and promoting their use (Marsden and Morley 2014) or using research to empower the disadvantaged (Badgett 2015) are obvious examples. Presumably for these academics, an agenda that values their aspiration to effect change may represent an additional bureaucratic hurdle when seeking research funding but it is not morally or professionally disturbing.

Some proponents of the impact agenda suggest that practitioners will be better placed to take decisions that achieve their goals if they utilise the cutting-edge insights into the physical world (science) and the social world (social science) provided by academic researchers. 'Practitioners' is used here to encompass policy-makers. By way of illustration, publicly funded research on genetics has opened up new avenues for exploring treatment possibilities. The commercial exploitation of this knowledge has resulted in improved idiosyncratic pharmacological interventions and, in turn, contributed to a thriving pharmaceutical sector. The most successful enterprises provide significant tax revenues and generate 'good quality' (well paid) employment. Publicly funded social science research that examines the corporate behaviour of commercially driven medical enterprises may lead to improved regulation, changes to fiscal policy and, perhaps, more effective laws to protect intellectual property. Simultaneously, it may find ways of remodelling the management and enhancing the organisational performance of the pharmaceutical firms.

This reasoning has great intuitive appeal. Who, after all, would want to conceal from practitioners, or public gaze, the results of publicly funded research of this kind? For many, this knowledge constitutes what economists call a 'public good', i.e. its availability to others is not diminished because of its consumption (or use) by one actor and no one is excluded from access to the knowledge. That some are able to 'exploit' it more than others is not inherently problematic. The poor channels of communication (market failures) between the producers of knowledge, in this case universities, and its consumers, namely businesses, public policy-makers and the public, can be overcome by public (research) policy interventions. Others might argue that a clearer focus on usability might overcome some of the waste associated with 'poor science' (Ioannidis 2014).

The dominance of this policy discourse in the UK (e.g. www.rcuk. ac.uk/innovation/impacts/) and in other developed economies (e.g.

Hicks 2012; OECD 2014; Watts 2017) has resulted in far greater attention being paid to the impact agenda by universities and individual academics. The principal policy change in recent years has been to move away from offering modest financial incentives to those who sought collaboration with external actors to a system of funding where there is an expectation of impact (Stern 2016).

In the UK, impact was defined officially as part of REF 2014 as follows: 'an effect on, change or benefit to the economy, society, culture, public policy or services, health, the environment or quality of life, beyond academia (emphasis added)'. Ratings varied from a 4 star 'Outstanding impacts in terms of their reach and significance' to an unclassified rating, which meant that 'The impact is of little or no reach and significance; or the impact was not eligible; or the impact was not underpinned by excellent research produced by the submitted unit' (www.ref.ac.uk). Similar language is used by others funding research, notably research councils. Chapter 4 provides an analysis of the relative impact of tourism research, including a consideration of the results of REF 2014.

An important challenge facing universities in the first instance, therefore, is to find ways of undertaking research that will be seen as relevant by others. This has excited significant academic controversy (see, for example, the recent debate between, inter alia, Dredge (2015) and Thomas (2015) on the need for relevance in academic policy research). It has been argued that there are tensions, and even fundamental incompatibilities, between the quest for impact and the research work of academics, even in subjects which have apparent vocational orientations such as business and management studies (e.g. Kieser and Leiner 2009, 2011; Kieser et al. 2015), planning (e.g. Bell 2007; Imrie 2009; Lovering 1999), sports management (e.g. Gerrard 2015) or tourism (e.g. Thomas 2011). There is evidence of resistance, usually in the form of papers that are critical of what is often termed the neoliberal turn in higher education (De Angelis and Harvie 2009; Fraser and Taylor 2016; Perry 2006; May and Perry 2011; Thomas 2012), but this has been slight, at least in its effect. Indeed, it has done little to counter the hegemonic discourse which is resulting in the elevation of two ideas: (i) that universities should inform the practices of practitioners, and (ii) that universities can influence these constituencies by undertaking 'appropriate' research and communicating their findings effectively.

COMPETITION, CONFORMITY
AND THE NEOLIBERAL UNIVERSITY

The diversity of the higher education sector both within and between countries represents one of the major challenges of undertaking a critical study of the kind reported in this book. It is obvious, even to those with no more than a passing interest, that not only have the number of universities increased substantially over recent decades but that university ownership (private or public), history, scale, status and missions vary substantially (for clear accounts of this complexity, historical development and implications, see Martin 2012; Watts 2017). Evidently, this makes generalisation very difficult. For the purposes of the analysis presented in this volume, the relevant constituency of universities is limited to those in pursuit of public funding to undertake research and operate within a performance-based funding regime. Such funding may take the form of specific project-based research awards or block grants based on periodic official departmental research assessment.

The complexity associated with defining modern universities is replicated when attempting to portray the higher education policy context that has spawned a concern with impact-driven research. Arguably, neoliberalism provides the most valuable descriptive and explanatory framework for understanding policy developments over recent decades. Notwithstanding the serious dangers arising from over-generalisation (Peck and Tickell 2007), Rustin (2016: 153) provides a useful summary of neoliberalism as follows:

> Neoliberalism, although it appears to name an ideology, is a term also used to refer to the entire post-1980s capitalist system which it dominates. This ideology is one which advocates free, unrestrained markets, and an ethic of individualism and individual choice, operating on a global scale.

As he goes on to point out, however:

> Its reality is somewhat different. The modern capitalist era is dominated not by free markets, free individual choice and individual entrepreneurs competing within them, but by global corporations, functioning as powerful oligopolies, and exercising a considerable degree of control over consumers, citizens and the political environment. These corporations ... are the entities whose profit-making operations dominate our world, and increasingly that of education.

The pervasive influence of neoliberalism on higher education policy has led to discourses that are characterised by the following: universities are engaged in global competition to attract students, staff and the income that they are able to gain in the form of fees and research grants; official audits of performance related to teaching, research, employment of graduates and many other domains enable 'consumers', via the metrics used to construct league tables, to make informed choices about quality and value; an approach to management is required which reflects those adopted by corporations (Buckland 2009; Hemsley-Brown and Oplatka 2010; Ayikoru et al. 2009).

Neoliberal universities are also seen as being embedded within regional, national and international economies. This usually involves describing their work in language that confirms their contribution to economic performance. Publicly funded research must, therefore, generate an impact which results in improved economic or social welfare if it is to be 'worthwhile' (Brown and Carasso 2015; Gaffikin and Perry 2009; Stern 2016).

The international marketisation of higher education has inspired a substantial body of work associated with managing modern universities 'effectively'. This literature 'recognises' the importance of differentiation to competitive success and asserts with confidence that the destiny of individual universities rests with its managers and academic staff; managers need to plan and invest strategically and the productivity of academics (research 'outputs', teaching quality and other aspects of their work) must keep pace with their competitors. From this perspective, some (poor) universities can be expected to fail while others ('the good ones') will flourish. Accordingly, authors such as Davis and Farrell (2016) explain how university managers need to position and brand their organisations to secure a prosperous future (see also Yudkevich et al. 2016, for a related discussion specifically in the context of seeking improved positions in global university rankings).

Some commentators have argued persuasively that modern corporate university governance threatens 'academic freedom' and weakens collegiality (Sayer 2015; Thomas 2005; Williams 2016). In addition to the work intensification associated with modern approaches to public management, there is a common suggestion that the apparently benign emphasis on meritocracy and transparency has also led to 'hyperindividualism' (Ryan 2012). The outcome of a shared understanding of 'achievement', and the availability of indicative metrics, results in self-aggrandisement for some (and the promise of career advancement) and a sense of failure for many (Clarke and Knights 2015). Moreover, the need to 'perform' creates a range of potentially damaging pressures, including those with an ethical dimension. There is a growing concern about data fabrication (Koczela et al. 2015), for example, and how the same data may be used in different, and barely compatible, ways by the same researchers to appeal to different audiences (Thomas 2005, 2010, 2017). Some of these issues are explored further in Chapter 5 where the discussion focuses on how some academic researchers in tourism and related areas have responded to working in neoliberal universities.

Many of those who are (quite reasonably) critical of contemporary higher education policy run the risk of fashioning caricatures of academic life and of being nostalgic for a mythical golden age (Docherty 2015). Martin (2012) provides a valuable historical sketch confirming the contrasting missions, both spatially and temporally, of universities internationally and the fluidity of the associated social contracts. His discussion reveals that the diversity and complexity of the contemporary university sector and the contests over their sociocultural roles are far from new. Further, the link made routinely between universities and economic performance is also shown to have a long lineage. Perhaps above all, critics of present-day higher education policy might acknowledge that universities have a centuries-old tradition of reproducing elites (Rustin 2016). Prestigious institutions, in particular, remain spaces for the socially privileged, regardless of contradictory pronouncements about access and social mobility (Baker 2014; Hemsley-Brown 2015). The 'credentials' and social networks acquired by those able to participate in elite education continue to provide them with significant material advantages in the labour market (Tholen et al. 2013).

There are numerous alternative ways proposed of organising universities (for a discussion of the evolution and competing normative conceptions of public universities, see Rustin 2016; and especially Watts 2017). Not surprisingly, many of these are associated with wider socio-economic critiques and perspectives on political economy. The concern here is not to take sides in these debates—not even in the debate about the desirability of research 'relevance'—but to examine the extent to which impact is achievable in marginal fields of enquiry and marginal sectors of the economy. The analysis of individual and organisational dynamics, in the academic and tourism sectorial spheres, suggests that it is not, even in the medium to long term. The implications of this analysis are considered in the final chapter.

WORKING AT THE MARGINS

Many will find it curious that sectors such as tourism are described as marginal when their economic and social significance suggests otherwise. According to recent estimates, tourism is one of the UK's largest economic sectors. Its contribution to GDP is approximately £126 billion (9%). Since 2010, it has been the fastest growing sector of the economy in terms of employment, accounting for almost 10% of total jobs (https://www.visitbritain.org/visitor-economy-facts). A study of the UK meetings industry, which might be seen as an important element of business tourism, found that its contribution to GDP was in the region of £60 billion per annum (MPI Foundation 2013). Socially, and culturally, holiday taking is also seen as important because it appears to make a positive contribution to well-being (Bos et al. 2015; Ferrer et al. 2016; McCabe 2015; McCabe and Johnson 2013).

In spite of occasional statements from prominent politicians, including the Prime Minister, tourism and its associated sectors are not treated as strategically important. There has been sustained lobbying over recent decades, for example, for tourism and events to be located within the ministry responsible for business and innovation. However, it has steadfastly remained within more marginal departments (smaller and far less influential), regardless of which political party or coalitions of parties have formed the government.

Since the late 1970s, there has been a growth in the number of students reading for tourism and, more latterly, event management degrees. They now form an established feature of the higher education landscape in the UK, represented by more than 100 universities educating some 30,000 students annually (Walmsley 2011a, b, 2012). Similar growth has been experienced elsewhere in the world though it appears to have faltered in some developed economies (Airey et al. 2015).

The routine inclusion of tourism and related subject associations in processes of policy consultation and governance arrangements confirms the legitimacy afforded to universities by policy-makers. Thus, policy-making networks and quasi-official lobbying groups in the UK such as the Tourism Alliance, the Business Visits and Events Partnership (BVEP), the Higher Education Academy (HEA) and the Quality Assurance Agency (QAA) (http://athe.org.uk/liaison/) all include the representatives of tourism academics, as well as other stakeholder groups.

There has been a progressive escalation of research activity which mirrors the maturity of tourism education. The catalogue of international journals is now extensive, with one recent estimate suggesting that there are almost 200 providing space for the dissemination of tourism research (www.ciret-tourism.com/index/listes_revues. html). Arguably, the most reputable of these are listed in the Chartered Association of Business Schools' 'The Academic Journal Guide' (www.charteredabs.org), a ranking system which now contains several 'elite' (world leading) peer-reviewed journals relating to tourism. Notwithstanding the crudeness of this and other ranking systems, the presence of tourism journals on such lists is read by many as a significant mark of academic legitimacy.

These credentials have not prevented some influential commentators from suggesting that tourism research is at the periphery of the research policy landscape. Lamenting the position of tourism research within the 2001 national research performance assessment, Tribe (2003: 233) noted that the exercise 'has neither rated tourism research highly nor has it offered tourism research funding commensurate with its extraordinary economic, social and cultural significance'. Several others have highlighted the historic marginalisation of tourism research in official research evaluation exercises and bemoaned the limited incidence of tourism research that is funded by research councils. Botterill (2002: 73), for example, has pointed out that the 'guidance notes on submissions to the RAE 2001 failed to mention 'tourism' at all ...' and Page (2003), a little later, concurred that tourism research lacked status when compared with more established disciplines.

The most recent official national assessment of research in the UK (2014) included tourism for the first time within the title of a Unit of Assessment. The unit was entitled Sport and Exercise Sciences, Leisure and Tourism (Unit 26). For many, this was seen—quite reasonably—as a coming of age. It certainly created a mechanism for those research centres deemed to be producing the highest quality work to receive funding alongside more established disciplines and fields. However, it is a telling reminder of the lack of a shared academic identity among tourism scholars that several institutions chose, because of the orientation of their work, to submit to Business and Management Studies (Unit 19) that makes no mention of tourism.

The sub-panel of Unit 26 that focused specifically on reviewing tourism research noted the following in their overview of the assessment:

Tourism research had improved noticeably since RAE2008 …. the panel was pleased to see greater and more effective engagement with theory and outputs with considerable methodological rigour. There was an increase in original, significant and rigorous overview papers reviewing the field and testament to the maturing nature and contribution of the subject area. The sub-panel also assessed world-leading tourism research that employed innovative methods of analysis of large and new datasets. The sub-panel was pleased to see a larger number of submissions from event management researchers (even though) …. this field is still at an earlier stage of maturity. (REF 2015: 117)

In spite of a significant number of contributions to Unit 19 (discussed in Chapter 4), the panel made no reference to tourism research in its review of business and management research.

Notwithstanding the legitimacy afforded to the field by the REF, it remains at the academic margins. With the exception of one university in the UK (Surrey), most departments of tourism are within teaching focused 'modern' (i.e. post 1992) universities; this is not a field that attracts the attention of research groups based at the twenty-four Russell Group of research-intensive universities (of which Surrey is not a member) (http://russellgroup.ac.uk/). Airey et al. (2015) suggest that the profile of the field is broadly similar elsewhere in the world.

This contrasts with other vocational fields, such as city and regional planning or management studies, which is studied at world leading universities. Arguably, this has an impact on the kind of academic staff that are attracted to the field. Indeed, it is noteworthy that there remains a suspicion, and patchy evidence, that academic staff in tourism and related fields are relatively less well qualified than their counterparts in more established disciplines (Wood 2015). The most recent data available from the Higher Education Statistical Agency (HESA) at the time of writing (February, 2018) indicate that in 2015/2016 slightly over a quarter (26%) of academic staff working in cost centres 'catering and hospitality management' had a doctorate as their highest qualification, compared with 50% in 'business and management' and 72% in 'geography and environmental studies'. Clearly, these do not align precisely with university departments but they probably confirm the broad observation about the academic credentials of those working in this field. Perhaps more than in other fields, there is also greater prevalence of academic managers adhering to the notion that academics require industrial experience if they are to be effective educators in tourism and related fields compared with others (Phelan et al. 2013).

A similar case may be made for the position of tourism research in Australia. Fewer tourism units of evaluation (UoEs) were submitted for scrutiny by universities in 2012 than previously, as university management chose to evaluate only those that were likely to score highly. The game playing of university strategists was probably rational because none of the tourism UoEs received the highest available rating in 2012 and the average rating was below most areas of business and management (Airey et al. 2015).

Other commonly used metrics reinforce the picture of a field that lags behind most of its academic counterparts. Peer-reviewed grant funding allocated to tourism projects by research councils is very low in the UK (0.5%) but is significantly worse in China and Australia (Airey et al. 2015).

Others have already considered the impact of research policy on marginalised groups. However, they have tended to challenge the diverting of research funding away from those with few resources or the narrowing of research questions to exclude the interests of those with little power (e.g. Fraser and Taylor 2016). Within these analyses, the academics are not marginal or marginalised. By contrast, the focus here is on a field of study that is considered marginal within academia and a sector of the economy that has little political influence (tourism).

It is generally accepted that one of the potential implications of a concern with strengthening the academic credentials of emerging fields is its simultaneous distancing from practice. The need to show theoretical sophistication and methodological rigour leads, arguably, to research questions that are removed from the concerns of practitioners. This appears to have happened in tourism studies. Drawing on a review of article titles from four leading journals, Hunt et al. (2014) suggest a decline in prominence of words which might be associated with impact, including 'industry', 'management', 'marketing' and 'planning'.

For reasons that will become clear in a moment, a brief consideration of the development of economics, a discipline that has a potentially close affinity with questions of practical policy-making, is instructive. Earle et al. (2017) express the dissatisfaction of many economists in their critique of the British economics curriculum, and by inference the influence this has on the kind of research undertaken, for its failure to address what many would consider to be routine questions for that discipline. The hegemony of neoclassical or new classical economics, where the emphasis is on acquiring the appropriate 'tools' of analysis, means that students are 'confronted with a series of abstract concepts and ideas that seem to have little to do with the actual economy' (Earle et al. 2017: 36).

Earle et al. (2017) go on to suggest that economics graduates emerging from world leading research-intensive universities are not required to understand the role and operation of major financial institutions such as the World Bank or the International Monetary Fund (IMF); to have identified the world's largest companies and how they behave; to know the size and form of the British economy in terms of measures such as wages, poverty, balance of trade, private debts, government deficits; to have gained a critical perspective on how official statistics are calculated; or to have assessed the causes of the 2008 financial crisis. The latter is perhaps most penetrating in illuminating the gap between the research and teaching of academic economists and its consequences because 'These models not only failed to foresee the possibility of such an event, but they were unable to explain it after it happened' (Earle et al. 2017: 68; see also, Desai 2015, for a systematic critique of this disciplinary crisis).

Whether academic economists obfuscate rather than illuminate is of little concern here. It shows, however, that the work of academics does not inevitably lead to the kind of knowledge construction that resonates with policy-makers or other practitioners. Part of the thesis advanced in this book is that the collective research output of tourism scholars has little to offer practitioners (or as much to offer as is claimed). This is not necessarily a criticism of the work of academic researchers but a questioning of the claims to relevance made increasingly by its producers. As Airey et al. (2015: 8) commented recently during their wide-ranging international review of the state of tourism education and research:

> In reality, links to the world of practice are generally poorly developed ... although the metrics are very imprecise and restricted, those that are available do not provide an encouraging picture for university management that their tourism departments are at the forefront in influencing their world.

The Argument Presented in This Book

This book examines research impact relating to the marginal fields of tourism and related academic subjects (these are taken to encompass event management and hospitality management). It draws on original data, a synthesis of previously published work and ethnographic reflections on *pro bono* and paid work for various organisations to argue that in marginal non-knowledge-intensive sectors of the economy, such as tourism, the knowledge produced by academics is largely irrelevant to practitioners. Moreover, for the reasons discussed in the book, this is unlikely to change. Funding academic research with an expectation of impact, therefore, represents a sub-optimal use of public money. The book concludes by calling for academic research in these contexts to be used far more for informing teaching and improving the quality of education offered to full-time and part-time students.

The second chapter explores the literature on innovation in tourism and related sectors, paying particular attention to the role of external knowledge in the innovation process. Influential conceptualisations of knowledge flows and innovation, notably absorptive capacity, are examined and a wide range of empirical evidence evaluated. This is followed by a brief review of mainstream theorising on public policy formation and a discussion of the factors influencing tourism policy chance. The chapter concludes by noting that universities do not feature prominently in most accounts of commercial innovation or policy change in tourism. Combined with other arguments developed in this book, it suggests that the potential for academic research to have a sustained—as opposed to sporadic—impact on innovation (and competitiveness) in tourism and other marginal sectors is very limited.

Professional associations are often considered to be valuable conduits for knowledge exchange between practitioners and universities. Their advocacy of professional standards, continuous professional development and 'best practice' resonates comfortably with statements universities make about research impact. Chapter 3 draws upon research into the professionalisation of occupations in tourism and events (Thomas and Thomas 2013, 2014), ESRC funded research on business engagement (RES-186-27-0015) and lessons learned from ESRC follow-on project funding (RES-189-25-0205), and reports ethnographic reflections on *pro bono* and paid work with the Institute of Travel and Tourism (ITT) and the Association of British Professional Conference Organisers (ABPCO). It argues that collaborative activity does not represent a stimulus for the promotion and utilisation of research insights for more effective practice (impact) but a benign harnessing of academic work to create stories for their members.

Chapter 4 reviews Thomas and Ormerod's (2017) study which traced the digital footprint of all tourism (and related) academics returned as part of a tourism submission to the REF in 2014. It compares commonly used indicators of academic quality (notably citations) with potential indicators of impact (such as citations by non-academics to academic work) to inform a discussion on the relative difference in non-academic impact between academics. REF impact templates and case studies, and data gathered from interviews with seventeen research-active academics and REF panel members, complement the analysis. Cases where academic researchers appear to have generated impact are revealed but these are rare, in spite of considerable collective effort. The chapter concludes by arguing that the findings are not explained by forms of market failure (that practitioners do not have access to or appreciate the value of academic work) but by recognising that universities, tourism businesses and tourism policy-makers operate within marginal and largely separate (but well defined) communities of practice.

The penultimate chapter considers the response to the impact agenda of academic researchers working in the marginal fields of tourism and related subjects. Drawing on interview data garnered from a selection of well-established researchers, it finds extensive evidence of individualistic career-related performativity and widespread participation in what others have called a 'new collegiality' (a system of control that emphasises competition with academics external to their workplace). Notwithstanding research orientations that often emphasise the economically liberating role of tourism, or its contribution to intercultural understanding and social improvement, there was little evidence of progressive or critical performativity. An important casualty of the growing focus on impact among those interviewed appears to be the reduced emphasis given to the teaching of students. This is argued to be damaging because it undermines a potentially more fruitful alternative activity, namely research to inform teaching.

REFERENCES

Airey, D., Tribe, J., Benckendorff, P., & Xiao, H. (2015). The managerial gaze: The long tail of tourism education and research. *Journal of Travel Research, 54*(2), 139–151.

Ayikoru, M., Tribe, J., & Airey, D. (2009). Reading tourism education: Neoliberalism unveiled. *Annals of Tourism Research, 36*(2), 191–202.

Badgett, M. V. L. (2015). *The public professor: How to use your research to change the world*. New York: New York University Press.

Baker, J. (2014). No Ivies, Oxbridge, or grandes écoles: Constructing distinctions in university choice. *British Journal of Sociology of Education, 35*(6), 914–932.

Banal-Estanol, A., Bonet-Jofre, M., & Lawson, C. (2015). The double-edged sword of industry collaboration: Evidence from engineering academics in the UK. *Research Policy, 44,* 1100–1175.

Bastow, S., Dunleavy, P., & Tinkler, J. (2014). *The impact of the social sciences.* London: Sage.

Bell, D. (2007). Fade to grey: Some reflections on policy and mundanity. *Environment and Planning A, 39,* 541–554.

Bos, L., McCabe, S., & Johnson, S. (2015). Learning never goes on holiday: An exploration of social tourism as a context for experiential learning. *Current Issues in Tourism, 18*(9), 859–875.

Botterill, D. (2002). Tourism studies and research quality assessment in UK universities. *Journal of Hospitality, Leisure, Sport and Tourism Education, 1*(2), 71–74.

Bozeman, B., Fay, D., & Slade, C. P. (2013). Research collaboration in universities and academic entrepreneurship: The state-of-the art. *Journal of Technology Transfer, 38,* 1–67.

Bozeman, B., Gaughan, M., Youtie, J., Slade, C. P., & Rimes, H. (2015). Research collaboration experiences, good and bad: Dispatches from the front lines. *Science and Public Policy.* https://doi.org/10.1093/scipol/scv035.

Bramwell, B., Higham, J., Lane, B., & Miller, G. (2016). Advocacy or neutrality? Disseminating research findings and driving change toward sustainable tourism in a fast changing world. *Journal of Sustainable Tourism, 24*(1), 1–7.

Brown, R., & Carassso, H. (2015). *Everything for sale? The marketization of UK higher education.* Abingdon: Routledge.

Buckland, R. (2009). Private and public sector models for strategies in universities. *British Journal of Management, 20,* 524–536.

Chartered Association of Business Schools (CABS). (2015). *The impact of business school research: Economic and social benefits.* London: CABS.

Clarke, C. A., & Knights, D. (2015). Careering through academia: Securing identities or engaging ethical subjectivities? *Human Relations, 68*(12), 1865–1888.

Davis, J. A., & Farrell, M. A. (2016). *The market oriented university. Transforming higher education.* Cheltenham: Edward Elgar.

De Angelis, M., & Harvie, D. (2009). 'Cognitive capitalism' and the rat-race: How capital measures immaterial labour in British universities. *Historical Materialism, 17,* 3–30.

Desai, M. (2015). *Hubris: Why economists failed to predict the crisis and how to avoid the next one.* New Haven: Yale University Press.

Docherty, T. (2015). *Universities at war.* London: Sage.

Dredge, D. (2015). Does relevance matter in academic policy research? *Journal of Policy Research in Tourism, Leisure and Events, 7*(2), 173–177.

Earle, J., Moran, C., & Ward-Perkins, Z. (2017). *The econocracy: The perils of leaving economics to the experts.* Manchester: Manchester University Press.

Ferrer, J. G., Ferrer, M. F., Ferrandis, E. D., McCabe, S., Garcia, J. S. (2016). Social tourism and healthy ageing. *International Journal of Tourism Research, 18*, 297–307.

Fraser, H., & Taylor, N. (2016). *Neoliberalization, universities and the public intellectual. Species, gender and class and the production of knowledge.* London: Palgrave Macmillan.

Gaffikin, F., & Perry, D. C. (2009). Discourses and strategic visions: The U.S. research university as an institutional manifestation of neoliberalism in a global era. *American Educational Research Journal, 46*(1), 115–144.

Gerrard, B. (2015). Rigour and relevance in sport management: Reconciling the competing demands of disciplinary research and user-value. *European Sport Management Quarterly, 15*(5), 505–515.

Hemsley-Brown, J. (2015). Getting into a Russell Group university: High scores and private schooling. *British Educational Research Journal, 41*(3), 398–422.

Hemsley-Brown, J., & Oplatka, I. (2010). Market orientation in universities. A comparative study of two national higher education systems. *International Journal of Educational Management, 24*(3), 204–220.

Hewitt-Dundas, N. (2012). Research intensity and knowledge transfer activity in UK universities. *Research Policy, 41*, 262–275.

Hicks, D. (2012). Performance-based university research funding systems. *Research Policy, 41*, 251–261.

Hunt, A. C., Gao, J., & Xue, L. (2014). A visual analysis of trends in the titles and keywords of top-ranked tourism journals. *Current Issues in Tourism, 17*(10), 849–855.

Imrie, R. (2009). The knowledge business in academic planning research. In F. Lo Piccolo & H. Thomas (Eds.), *Ethics and planning research* (pp. 71–89). Farnham: Ashgate.

Ioannidis, J. P. (2014). How to make more published research true. *PLoS Medicine, 11*(10), e1001747.

Kieser, A., & Leiner, L. (2009). Why the rigour-relevance gap in management research is unbridgeable. *Journal of Management Studies, 46*(3), 516–533.

Kieser, A., & Leiner, L. (2011). On the social construction of relevance: A rejoinder. *Journal of Management Studies, 48*(4), 891–898.

Kieser, A., Nicolaib, A., & Seidlc, D. (2015). The practical relevance of management research: Turning the debate on relevance into a rigorous scientific research program. *The Academy of Management Annals, 9*(1), 143–233.

Koczela, S., Furlong, C., McCarthy, J., & Mushtaq, A. (2015). Curbstoning and beyond: Confronting data fabrication in survey research. *Statistical Journal of the IAOS (International Association for Official Statistics), 31*(3), 413–422.

Lovering, J. (1999). Theory led by policy: The inadequacies of the 'new regionalism' (illustrated from the case of Wales). *International Journal of Urban and Regional Research, 23*(2), 379–395.

Marchant, P. (2017). Why lighting claims might be wrong. *International Journal of Sustainable Lighting, 19,* 69–74.

Marsden, T., & Morley, A. (Eds.). (2014). *Sustainable food systems: Building a new paradigm.* London: Routeldge.

Martin, B. R. (2012). Are universities and university research under threat? Towards an evolutionary model of university speciation. *Cambridge Journal of Economics, 36*(3), 543–565.

May, T., & Perry, B. (2011). Universities, reflexivity and critique: Uneasy parallels in practice. *Policy Futures in Education, 11*(5), 505–514.

McCabe, S. (2015). Family leisure, opening a window on the meaning of family. *Annals of Leisure Research, 18*(2), 175–179.

McCabe, S., & Johnson, S. (2013). The happiness factor in tourism: Subjective well-being and social tourism. *Annals of Tourism Research, 41,* 42–65.

Meeting Professionals International (MPI) Foundation. (2013). *The economic impact of the UK meeting and event industry.* Dallas: MPI.

Organisation for Economic Cooperation and Development (OECD). (2014). *OECD science, technology and industry outlook 2014.* Paris: OECD.

Page, S. J. (2003). Evaluating research performance in tourism: The UK experience. *Tourism Management, 24,* 607–622.

Park, K., Phillips, W. J., Canter, D. D., & Abbot, J. (2011). Hospitality and tourism research rankings by author, university and country using six major journals: The first decade of the new millennium. *Journal of Hospitality and Tourism Research, 35*(3), 381–416.

Peck, J., & Tickell, A. (2007). Conceptualising neoliberalism, thinking Thatcherism. In J. Leitner, J. Peck, & E. Sheppard (Eds.), *Contesting neoliberalism: Urban frontiers* (pp. 26–50). New York: Guildford Press.

Perry, B. (2006). Science, society and the university: A paradox of values. *Social Epistemology, 20*(3–4), 201–219.

Phelan, K. V., Mejia, C., & Hertzman, J. (2013). The industry experience gap; hospitality faculty perceptions of the importance of faculty industry experience. *Journal of Hospitality and Tourism Education, 25,* 123–130.

Research Excellence Framework (REF). (2015). Research Excellence Framework 2014: Overview report by Main Panel C and Sub-panels 16 to 26. http://www.ref.ac.uk/media/ref/content/expanel/member/Main%20Panel%20C%20overview%20report.pdf.

Rustin, M. (2016). The neoliberal university and its alternatives. *Soundings: Spaces of Resistance, 63,* 147–170.

Ryan, S. (2012). Academic zombies: A failure of resistance or a means of survival? *Australian Universities Review, 54*(2), 3–11.

Sayer, D. (2015). *Rank hypocrisies: The insult of the REF*. London: Sage.

Severt, D., Tesone, D., Bottorff, T., & Carpenter, M. (2009). A world ranking of the top 100 hospitality and tourism program. *Journal of Hospitality and Tourism Research, 33*(4), 451–470.

Stern, L. N. (2016). *Building on success and learning from experience: An independent review of the Research Excellence Framework*. London: Department for Business, Energy and Industrial Strategy.

Tholen, G., Brown, P., Power, S., & Allouch, A. (2013). The role of networks and connections in educational elites' labour market entrance. *Research in Social Stratification and Mobility, 34*, 142–154.

Thomas, H. (2005). Pressures, purpose and collegiality in UK planning education. *Planning Theory and Practice, 6*(2), 238–247.

Thomas, H. (2010). Knowing the city: Local coalitions, knowledge and research. In C. Allen & R. Imrie (Eds.), *The knowledge business* (pp. 77–92). Farnham: Ashgate.

Thomas, H. (2012). Values and the planning school. *Planning Theory, 11*, 400–417.

Thomas, H. (2015). Does relevance matter in academic policy research? A comment on Dredge. *Journal of Policy Research in Tourism, Leisure and Events, 7*(2), 178–182.

Thomas, H. (2017). Framing turbulence in the academy: UK planning academics in a period of change. *Town Planning Review, 88*(5), 557–577.

Thomas, R. (2011). Academics as policy-makers: (Not) Researching tourism and events policy from the inside. *Current Issues in Tourism, 14*(6), 493–506.

Thomas, R., & Ormerod, N. (2017). The (almost) imperceptible impact of tourism research on policy and practice. *Tourism Management, 62*, 379–389.

Thomas, R., & Thomas, H. (2013). What are the prospects for professionalizing events management in the UK? *Tourism Management Perspectives, 6*, 8–14.

Thomas, R., & Thomas, H. (2014). 'Hollow from the start?' Professional associations and the professionalization of tourism in the UK. *The Service Industries Journal, 34*(1), 38–55.

Tribe, J. (2003). The RAE-ification of tourism research in the UK. *International Journal of Tourism Research, 5*, 225–234.

Walmsley, A. (2011a). *AEME report on events higher education in the UK, 2011*. Association for Events Management Education.

Walmsley, A. (2011b). *CHME report on hospitality higher education in the UK, 2011*. Council for Hospitality Management Education.

Walmsley, A. (2012). *Tourism intelligence Monitor: ATHE report on tourism higher education in the UK, 2012*. Association for Tourism in Higher Education.

Watermeyer, R. (2016). Impact in the REF: Issues and obstacles. *Studies on Higher Education, 41*(2), 199–214.

Watts, R. (2017). *Public universities, managerialism and the value of higher education.* London: Palgrave Macmillan.

Williams, J. (2016). *Academic freedom in an age of conformity.* London: Palgrave Macmillan.

Wood, R. (2015). 'Folk' understandings of quality in UK higher hospitality education. *Quality Assurance in Education, 23*(4), 236–338.

Yudkevich, M., Altbach, P. G., & Rumbley, L. E. (2016). *The global academic rankings game: Changing institutional policy, practice and academic life.* Abingdon: Routledge.

CHAPTER 2

Knowledge Flows and Innovation in Marginal Sectors: Do Universities Matter?

... but I think the majority of the work they (practitioners) were given they didn't take away and utilise. Some did but the majority did not. And I'm not quite sure why ... I think that might be the nature of tourism.
Research professor interviewed for this book

Abstract This chapter explores the literature on innovation in tourism and related sectors, paying particular attention to the role of external knowledge in the innovation process. Influential conceptualisations of knowledge flows and innovation, notably absorptive capacity, are explored and a wide range of empirical evidence evaluated. This is followed by a brief review of mainstream theorising on public policy formation and a discussion of the factors influencing tourism policy chance. The chapter concludes by noting that universities do not feature prominently in most accounts of commercial innovation or policy change in tourism. Combined with other arguments developed in this book, it suggests that the potential for academic research to have a sustained— as opposed to sporadic—impact on innovation (and competitiveness) in tourism and other marginal sectors is very limited.

Keywords Tourism studies · Competitiveness · Research

© The Author(s) 2018
R. Thomas, *Questioning the Assessment of Research Impact*, Palgrave Critical University Studies,
https://doi.org/10.1007/978-3-319-95723-4_2

INTRODUCTION

Research policy in the UK, and in other countries that operate performance-based research funding systems, rewards universities that are able to demonstrate the impact of their research on practitioners and other policy-makers. Several specific funding initiatives are used to encourage collaboration between universities and practitioners. These range from research council funded business placement fellowships, whereby academic researchers spend time in a company, to knowledge transfer partnerships (KTPs) which involve companies appointing an 'associate' who works in the company and is supervised by a university tutor (resulting in the award of a research degree) (for more information, see https://www.gov.uk/guidance/knowledge-transfer-partnerships-what-they-are-and-how-to-apply).

The precise details of the schemes are of limited importance for the purposes of this chapter. What matters here is that they all start from the same premise; according to official accounts, businesses, non-governmental organisations (NGOs) and public agencies will, *inter alia*, become more innovative and improve their performance (usually framed in economic terms and described as competitiveness) if they collaborate with universities. There is, with reason, a widely held view that innovation leads to improved performance (e.g. Martinez-Roman et al. 2015). Whether gaining access to the knowledge produced in universities leads to innovation is much less certain.

The politically marginal nature of tourism as a field of enquiry and policy domain is reflected in official promotion of research impact-related funding initiatives. Even a cursory glance at the web pages of government departments concerned with business and the economy, for example, reveals the centrality of science, technology, engineering and mathematics (STEM) in official thinking (see, for example, www.innovateuk.gov.uk). Periodic research performance evaluations such as the Research Excellence Framework (REF) do not, however, generally distinguish between disciplines or sectors, apart from in levels of funding. The expectation is that the more successful research centres will demonstrate the impact of their research on policy and practice.

This chapter provides a critical assessment of the policy rationale invoked by higher education funding agencies for including impact as part of their performance evaluations. It does so by reviewing explanations for contrasting levels and patterns of innovation in tourism. Studies that examine university–industry and university–policy-maker collaborations are excluded from the discussion because they begin with universities as a central focus. Such studies are considered later in the book. This chapter will show that the most prominent explanations for why some firms are innovative and others are not, or why novel public policy emerges in certain places or at certain times, do not usually mention the potential contribution of universities in their explanatory schema. Where they do, they are incidental. By current accounts, innovative organisations do not require universities in order to innovate. This calls into question the potential value of tourism (and other) researchers investing time and effort in their quest for research impact.

'Competitiveness' is a complex and multifaceted notion and perhaps especially so when considered in the context of destinations. Abreu-Novais et al. (2015) show how various contributors use the term and discuss key factors that are claimed to influence levels of competitiveness. Two constituent aspects of competitiveness are common to most accounts. The first relates to the extent to which local businesses and other organisations relevant to the tourism offer, such as publicly funded attractions, are entrepreneurial and innovative. The second is the importance attached to the role of public policy-makers in creating the conditions whereby tourism can flourish. This too implies an ability to be innovative. In this chapter, therefore, the term competitiveness is used loosely to refer to the behaviour of commercial and non-commercial organisations, or collections of organisations in specified locations (destinations), that are innovative and then go on to improve their (business) performance.

DEFINING AND THEORISING INNOVATION IN TOURISM

'Innovation' suffers from being defined in a multitude of ways. Hall and Williams (2008: 5) utilise Kanter's (1983), noting that it is 'the process of bringing any new, problem solving idea into use'. Central to this definition are ideas of adaptability and change within organisations. Innovations may relate to products or services, processes or managerial practices (Hjalager 2010). Moreover, as others have noted, 'As long as the idea is perceived as new to the people involved, it is an "innovative idea", even though it may appear to others to be an "imitation" of something that exists elsewhere' (Van de Ven et al. 2008: 9).

The consequences of innovations, therefore, may be radical, in the sense that they transform practices or even markets, or represent modest, incremental, adaptations (Hjalager 2002).

A recent highly regarded comprehensive review of the literature captures the essence of innovation and its link to creativity by proposing the following definition:

> Creativity and innovation at work are the process, outcomes and products of attempts to develop and introduce new and improved ways of doing things. The creativity stage of this process refers to idea generation, and innovation refers to the subsequent stage of implementing ideas towards better procedures, practices or products. Creativity and innovation can occur at the level of the individual, work team, organisation or at more than one of these levels combined but will invariably result in identifiable benefits at one or more of these levels of analysis. (Anderson et al. 2014: 1298)

Ryu and Lee (2016) identify six types of innovation typically associated with organisations in the service sector—those relating to products, processes, delivery, strategy, management and marketing. Estimates of the scale and patterns of innovation in tourism vary (cf. Hertog et al. 2011; Orfila-Sintes et al. 2005). This is not surprising; the corollary of a failure to agree on definitions is diverging opinions on what indicators should be used in empirical studies to measure aspects of innovation (e.g. Arta and Acob 2003; Hjalager and Flagestad 2012; Sorensen 2007; Carlisle et al. 2013). On the other hand, there is a degree of consensus among researchers that understanding organisational-level behaviour is an essential first step to being able to comprehend, and perhaps influence, aggregate innovation at a local, regional or national destination level (Cooke et al. 2011).

Most scholars of innovation now acknowledge the importance of sectorial context (e.g. Autio et al. 2014; Garud et al. 2014; Vega-Jurado et al. 2008) and seek to accommodate this concern in their work. Perhaps the most noteworthy structural characteristic of the tourism sector is the high incidence of small and medium-sized enterprises (SMEs). This, of course, contributes to its political marginalisation (Thomas 2007). The high level of informality associated with such businesses and the personalised manner in which they are managed represent two of the critical—if often conveniently overlooked—conceptual differences between large manufacturing firm and tourism SMEs (Díaz-Chao et al.

2016; Kallmuenzer and Peters 2018; Thomas et al. 2011). Studies conducted within large bureaucratic manufacturing concerns—common in studies of innovation—will, therefore, be of very limited value to those interested in tourism organisations.

Secondly, the organisation of large tourism businesses differs from even comparably sized enterprises in manufacturing. Travel agents or tour operators typically create packages that are provided by a variety of contractually flexible suppliers. Others in the sector, e.g. professional events agencies, employ numerous freelance staff on a regular but short-term basis even if they present themselves as having 'global reach' (McCabe 2009; Weber and Ladkin 2009). These relatively weak employment ties allow flexibility (Rogers 2013) but may also bring into question the explanatory power of current innovation models; by way of illustration, the common emphasis on the work of research and development (R&D) departments sits uncomfortably within tourism where any R&D function is incorporated much more loosely across the business (to the extent that the notion becomes meaningless).

Finally, the valuing of knowledge in tourism contrasts sharply with knowledge-intensive industries. The extensive literature on knowledge management and knowledge networks in tourism (e.g. Cooper 2006; Czernek 2017; Jacob et al. 2014; Reinl and Kelliher 2010, 2014; Shaw and Williams 2009) shows that acquiring technical or non-technical formal knowledge is not seen as a primary means of gaining competitive advantage by many practitioners. Instead, the flow of tacit knowledge within familiar and relatively unsophisticated networks is seen as far more important by the actors (Thomas 2012; Li et al. 2017).

Martinez-Roman et al. (2015) point out that the literature on innovation in tourism can be divided into those that adapt mainstream theories to interrogate innovation in tourism and those that emphasise the need to develop context-specific theory (e.g. Alsos et al. 2014). This chapter draws upon both selectively in an attempt to overcome some of the major failings of each. One of the most common weaknesses of the latter is that it does not take account of the sophisticated theoretical and empirical advances made in the innovation literature. As a result, it may be contextually rich but runs the risk of being theoretically underdeveloped.

Anderson et al. (2014) consider several prominent theoretical perspectives on innovation that have been influential in management research over the past decade. These encompass componential theory of organisational innovation, reflecting the legacy of contributors such as Amabile

(1997) who have shown how work environments influence creativity at work, to models of individual creative actions reflecting the early work of researchers such as Ford (1996) and, more latterly, Unsworth and Clegg (2010). Interactionist perspectives (e.g. Zhou and Shalley 2010) have also been utilised and some have theorised the role culture (e.g. Stahl et al. 2009).

Current theorising suggests that organisational innovation is influenced by several 'determinant factors' (Tejada and Moreno 2013) or 'drivers of innovation' (Hall and Williams 2008), including technology, competition, innovation systems, management and public policy (Chen 2011; Hall 2009; Kianto et al. 2017; Ottenbacher 2007; Pittaway et al. 2004; Smith et al. 2008). Hjalager (2002) provides a much quoted categorisation of determinants of innovative capability at the level of the firm: (i) access to knowledge; (ii) organisation of resources by managers; and (iii) the availability of appropriate 'human capital' and the culture within which people operate. Martinez-Roman et al. (2015) extend the notion of innovative capability to include the business context (e.g. its size and access to funding) and the competitive and institutional environment within which it operates. Recent research on innovation in destinations has emphasised the role of relational trust, network position, boundary spanning and knowledge sharing as central features of innovation (Zach and Hill 2017). Almost all of the conceptual and empirical studies referred to above exclude universities from their explanatory schema. There is little to suggest that universities represent an important element of the innovative process at any scale. Indeed, Martinez-Roman et al. (2015) found that the employment of graduates, which are sometimes seen as a channel for knowledge transfer, might even stifle innovation.

Of greater potential interest for the purposes of this book is the role that the acquisition and utilisation of external knowledge play in innovation (Scott et al. 2008; Shaw and Williams 2009; Xiao and Smith 2006), particularly because tourism businesses invest comparatively little in research and development (Williams and Shaw 2011). This reflects a widely accepted suggestion in the literature that the capacity of organisations to identify, collect and use external information for innovative purposes is a cornerstone of organisational innovation (Cooper 2006; Zahra and George 2002). Consistent with this, Lopez-Vega et al. (2016: 125) demonstrated recently that organisational search behaviours vary in sophistication and that these have consequences for likely innovation.

The knowledge produced by universities may, *prima facie* at least, have a potentially positive role to play in supporting the innovation of tourism organisations and is worthy of further consideration.

KNOWLEDGE AND INNOVATION: ABSORPTIVE CAPACITY

There has been an 'avalanche of interest' (West et al. 2014: 805) over the past decade or more in ideas of open innovation (Chesbrough 2003). The resulting literature suggests that innovative organisations tend to secure new knowledge via collaboration with external actors (Laursen and Salter 2014). Access is enabled relationally via informal and formal networks which often involve reciprocity of value (Ritala et al. 2015). There is a *prima facie* case to be made for seeing universities as a potential source of knowledge for these outward-looking organisations; universities—it could be argued—might achieve research impact by becoming part of the knowledge networks of tourism organisations in the public and private sectors.

Absorptive capacity, or the ability of an organisation to acquire, assimilate, transform and exploit external knowledge for competitive purposes is an influential strand of this literature. Indeed, as Lane et al. (2006: 833) have argued, absorptive capacity represents 'one of the most important constructs to emerge in organisational research in recent decades'. Absorptive capacity has been summarised as follows:

> ....(absorptive capacity) refers to one of a firm's fundamental learning processes: its ability to identify, assimilate, and exploit knowledge from the environment. These three dimensions encompass not only the ability to imitate other firms' products or processes but also the ability to exploit less commercially focused knowledge, such as scientific research. Developing and maintaining absorptive capacity is critical to a firm's long term survival and success because absorptive capacity can reinforce, complement, or refocus the firm's knowledge base. (Lane et al. 2006: 833)

The development of absorptive capacity is usually attributed to Cohen and Levinthal (1990), though other prominent scholars have offered significant theoretical refinements. Zahra and George (2002), for example, claim four dimensions of absorptive capacity, namely acquisition, assimilation, transformation and exploitation. The first two are categorised by them as 'potential absorptive capacity' and the latter as 'realised'.

Knowledge acquisition will be affected by the intensity, scale and scope of activity, and will often be prompted by a trigger such as increased competition or a declining market. As others have shown, the characteristics of the activation trigger will condition the organisation's reaction (Van de Ven et al. 2008). Assimilation of knowledge refers to an organisation's capability to interpret knowledge for strategic purposes. The third capability is one which enables new knowledge to be combined with existing knowledge from within the organisation and results in novel understanding. As Zahra and George (2002: 190) argue, 'the ability of firms to recognize two apparently incongruous sets of information and then combine them to arrive at a new schema represents a transformation capability ... It yields new insights ... (and alters how) ... the firm sees itself and its competitive landscape'. 'Exploitation' is the creation of procedural mechanisms in order to exploit new knowledge for the purposes of innovation (Easterby-Smith et al. 2008).

Mechanisms for sharing knowledge are required if absorptive capacity is to be realised. This may be challenging because a variety of structural, cognitive, behavioural and political barriers may act as inhibitors. Some have argued that organisational power and/or seniority tends to play a positive role in knowledge acquisition but that episodic power, or that which emerges from coalitions of interests and at particular times, is critical to the effective exploitation of knowledge (Easteby-Smith et al. 2008). There is some empirical evidence to suggest that formal knowledge sharing mechanisms are somewhat more effective than informal ones. Moreover, an organisation's ability to integrate knowledge and to 'learn' from past experience, alongside a flexible approach to human resource management, appears to help explain contrasting performance between organisations or differences over time within organisations (Chang et al. 2013; Wang et al. 2018).

Most prominent conceptualisations of absorptive capacity consider 'regimes of appropriability'. This refers to an ability to retain competitive advantage by making it difficult for others to imitate the innovation emerging as a consequence of having high levels of absorptive capacity (Laursen and Salter 2014). Typically, researchers discuss 'isolating mechanisms' (e.g. secrecy) as a means of limiting knowledge spillovers but because of the structural characteristics of the tourism sector—leading to high levels of temporary employment and high labour turnover (Rogers 2013)—this is likely to be limited in its effectiveness. Indeed, as innovation in tourism is usually fairly easy to replicate and often have their antecedents outside the sector (e.g. from technology businesses), creating effective regimes of appropriability is not likely to yield much more than a short-term advantage and is, therefore, not particularly significant (Hjalager 2015).

Even though there is a general acceptance that knowledge acquisition and use are linked to an organisation's ability to innovate (Cooper 2006; Dwyer and Edwards 2009; Fosfuri and Tribo 2008; Gallego et al. 2013; Scott et al. 2008; Shaw and Williams 2009; Xiao and Smith 2007), very few rigorous empirical studies of absorptive capacity in tourism have been conducted (Shaw 2015; Chen 2011; Nieves and Segarra-Cipress 2015). This is surprising because some have argued that knowledge derived from outside the organisation is especially important in this sector (King et al. 2014; Williams and Shaw 2011). This may be because tourism businesses tend to function with open systems of innovation, i.e. instead of investing in research and development (R&D) departments, they utilise the knowledge of suppliers, customers and their business networks (Laursen and Salter 2014; Mina et al. 2014; West et al. 2014; Nieves and Segarra-Cipres 2015). As Vega-Jurado, Gutierrez-Garcia and Fernandez-de-Lucio (2009) have shown, however, greater in-house technological capability means that enterprises are more likely and able to take advantage of access to potentially valuable external knowledge.

Thomas and Wood (2014, 2015) are among the only academics to have provided theoretical advancement of absorptive capacity following research among tourism businesses. Drawing on data gathered from interviews with senior practitioners in innovative organisations, and a survey of members of a leading international practitioner association, Thomas and Wood (2015) used structural equation modelling to show that the four-factor model of absorptive capacity so prominent in the innovation literature is inadequate when applied to business in tourism or—as they showed in an earlier study—the hotel sector (Thomas and Wood 2014). Figure 2.1 provides a representation of their most recent conceptualisation.

Thomas and Wood (2015) show that activation triggers and prior experience (learning) become significant once knowledge acquisition—usually gained via personal networks—has occurred. In other words, businesses tend not to utilise acquired knowledge effectively for innovative purposes until they are stimulated to do so by events (activation triggers). The business practices of those they studied also resonated with theoretically emerging notions of 'reciprocity' (Ritala et al. 2015),

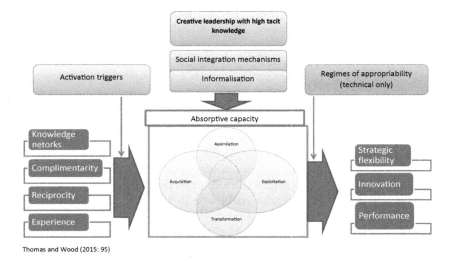

Thomas and Wood (2015: 95)

Fig. 2.1   A model of absorptive capacity in tourism   (*Source* Thomas and Wood 2015: 95)

'commitment-trust' (Hashim and Tan 2015) and 'familiarity' (Zheng and Yang 2015). For example, organisations would share freely with competitors, knowledge about contracts they had secured because they knew that they could not be won again (e.g. the hosting of a major convention). The incentive for this 'openness' was an anticipated reciprocity from those within their network.

The data analysed by Thomas and Wood (2015) demonstrated the importance of creative, personalised and experienced leadership (with high tacit knowledge of the sector). The role of management practices identified by Amabile et al. (1996) as a vital component of a creative organisation also appears to pertain to tourism organisations (see also Anderson et al. 2014). Perhaps predictably, an organisational culture of sharing knowledge, especially when formalised, was important to the innovation process because it encouraged and enabled the transformation and exploitation of knowledge. The data suggest that managers in tourism organisations—unlike those in manufacturing—have a more direct influence and participate more actively in the iterative processes of acquiring, assimilating, transforming and exploiting knowledge for organisational gain. Thus, knowledge acquisition, assimilation, transformation and exploitation are represented in Fig. 2.1 as overlapping. The close proximity of senior practitioners to their employees and to the market, even in relatively large tourism businesses, suggests that they act as a bridge between acquired knowledge and innovation more than in other sectors.

The brief review of the literature provided above does not constitute a theoretically sophisticated or empirically comprehensive assessment of absorptive capacity in tourism. Readers are invited to read the sources cited if that is their aspiration. The discussion does, however, illustrate very clearly the manner in which universities are not written in to accounts of why some organisations are more innovative and competitive than others even when external knowledge is at centre stage. For businesses, therefore, universities are largely irrelevant and the knowledge they produce is not likely to be in great demand or generate significant impact. Because of the widely documented importance of personal networks to knowledge flows and the relational nature of knowledge acquisition in tourism, the next section considers this issue in the context of tourism. It draws heavily of a project funded by the ESRC and reported in Thomas (2012).

PERSONAL NETWORKS, KNOWLEDGE FLOWS AND PRACTITIONER LEARNING

Hjalager (2002) provides a valuable overview of the processes by which knowledge flows occur in tourism. These are what she terms the trade system (access to best practice, market research or certification), the infrastructural system (notably relating to transport), the regulatory system (including legal interventions on the environment, employment and consumer law) and the technological system. Weidenfeld et al. (2010) develop her work by introducing firm-level (such as inter-firm exchanges) and individual-level mechanisms. The latter is discussed in this section.

An alternative approach to investigating organisational innovation and competitiveness, and relationships with knowledge acquisition and use, is to focus on the key actors within organisations. Active participation in networks represents one of the most prominent examples of an activity that is cited regularly as a common source of knowledge in tourism (Scott and Ding 2008; Baggio and Cooper 2010; Presenza and Cipollina

2010). Social relationships are pivotal in these 'knowledge networks' prompting some commentators to suggest that the management of relationships has, in many respects, become as important as the management of organisations (Beesley 2005; Inkpen and Tsang 2005). The literature on how managers acquire and use knowledge—which emphasise a tendency to rely on personal rather than impersonal sources (Cross et al. 2001; Xiao and Smith 2009)—corroborate observations made about the importance of networks to knowledge transfer.

A valuable, though surprisingly neglected, approach to adding theoretical rigour to an understanding of the process of knowledge acquisition is to examine how practitioners and policy-makers learn (Beamish 2005; Sherlock and Nathan 2008). Informed by Mezirow's (1991, 2000, 2003, 2009) work on adult learning, Thomas (2012) examined learning among senior practitioners in commercial tourism organisations. Briefly, for Mezirow (2009: 22), adult learning 'may be understood as the process of using a prior interpretation to construe a new or revised interpretation of the meaning of one's experience to guide future action'. Interpretation occurs within an individual's frame of reference, which—in turn—is divided between 'habits of mind' and 'points of view'. Gunnlaugson (2007: 136) explains the difference succinctly as follows:

> Habits of mind are deeply embedded assumptions that we hold, and a point of view is an outward perspective that we take in response to a given life-world situation or set of circumstances … our point of view emerges from our habits of mind, which are more deeply woven into our character, worldview, and habitual ways of interpretation.

For Mezirow, learning takes place in several interconnected ways that extend existing subjective meanings or existing frames of reference by the creation of new meanings. Learning may also, however, be more radical whereby assumptions are questioned leading to changes of perspective. A shift from seeing email activity during vacations as a sign of commitment to signifying something else (perhaps a failure to delegate) illustrates the point.

Finally, frames of reference may be challenged and changed (transformational learning), perhaps via the acquisition of knowledge or alterations to circumstances. For example, being made redundant may lead to a questioning of an individual's sense of identity associated with work (Mezirow 2009; Sherlock and Nathan 2008). According to this perspective, a dialectical process, therefore, results in individuals learning by interpreting events against existing expectations. A reluctance to create new meanings is a critical constraint to transformational learning. This obtains because actors 'are able to select how they inform themselves ... (and) ... can ensure that they are not confronted by new ideas. Mezirow talks of people being trapped in their meaning perspective and unable to develop' (Moon 2002: 109). Presumably, practitioners who might be described in these terms are unlikely to gravitate towards universities as sources of new knowledge.

In a study of knowledge flows in tourism, Thomas (2012) found that the Chief Executive Officers and/or Directors of major international tourism businesses that he interviewed adopted a relatively unsophisticated informal approach to their own learning. While external sources of information were important, their form—and how they were used—was typical of those used by actors holding much more junior positions or those that ran their own (small) businesses (Scott and Ding 2008; Xiao and Smith 2009). The emphasis tended to be on what academics might define as superficial sources such as the trade press because of their immediacy, brevity and obvious relevance.

Formal and informal relationships developed outside the organisation represented a prominent feature of the accounts of their own learning given by participants (Thomas 2012). The key considerations for senior practitioners were that members of their network operated in the same 'world', or community of practice, which implied shared interest and values, an epistemological unity and mutually respectful and trusting relationships. Truth claims tended to be tested with these considerations in mind. In other words, the most important people from whom they learned were like themselves.

In Thomas's (2012) study, senior practitioners seemed to emphasise instrumental learning, i.e. that which was required to address particular problems (Mezirow 2003). This should not be taken to imply a lack of reflection; habits of mind and points of view formed frames of reference within which participants undertook their reflection. As a result, learning tended to extend meanings or frames of reference by the creation of new meanings. There was little evidence that Thomas (2012) could find of reframing or transformational learning.

Universities represent an extremely marginal source of knowledge for all of those interviewed, notably for its tourism or related research (there is a greater openness to business 'gurus' and dissemination in publications such as the Harvard Business Review). Knowledge of tourism research was patchy at best. However, the data did not suggest an objection in principle to working with universities.

For some, perhaps many, the study implies that universities should spend time engendering positive relationships with decision-makers and negotiating access to their networks. This will involve adopting the language of business and positioning 'solutions' in terms that are clear and accessible (which need not mean simplistic). Although this interpretation has intuitive appeal, especially for those seeking to make a case for the use of academic research among practitioners, a more critical reading of the data leads to a different conclusion. If those managing large commercial tourism organisations learn within their own 'meaning perspectives', the enterprises they lead are not likely to be knowledge-driven organisations with high absorptive capacity that would be susceptible to collaborative learning with universities.

It is not surprising business leaders would not see universities as obvious or, even particularly, helpful sources of knowledge. The constituencies to which they belong can be seen as distinct communities of practice, where powerful value systems operate that inevitably undermine the aspiration of common ways of 'seeing' with those working in universities as academic researchers. Obviously, there is also heterogeneity within these 'communities' but prominent notions of relevance and practicality transcend differences. These are at odds with research practices which, to gain academic status, are destined increasingly to become abstract (Hall 2011).

Publicly funded initiatives to support (incentivise) engagement between businesses and research-active academics in tourism will increase the amount of collaboration. Indeed, the British Economic and Social Research Council's (ESRC) follow-on funding scheme, for example, enabled the research reported in Thomas (2012) to be used for interesting collaborative work with the Institute of Travel and Tourism (ITT) (see also Chapter 3). However, because such funding arrangements do not, and arguably cannot, alter the dynamics of the relationships between universities and businesses, they offer little prospect of creating impact over anything other than the short term; and even that is questionable. Finally, although not developed here, the misplaced emphasis on market failure probably applies even more acutely in the context of small businesses where the benefits of working with universities are also assumed to exist but not usually demonstrated (Thomas et al. 2011).

IDEAS, EVIDENCE AND POLICY FORMATION (OR FADS AND FASHIONS IN PUBLIC POLICY)

If attention is switched from understanding factors that influence innovation and competitiveness in the private sector to related issues in the context of tourism policy-making, a similarly marginal role for academics and academic research is revealed. John's (2012: 1) highly regarded review of public policy studies begins with a clear statement of purpose:

> Research on public policy seeks to explain how decision makers, working within or close to the machinery of government and other political institutions, produce public actions that are intended to have an impact outside the political system.

In addition to a systematic review of the prominent theoretical perspectives most often drawn upon to explain policy formation, John (2012) argues for the importance of ideas, and their flow within the political system, in an explanatory schema. While acknowledging that ideas permeate most rational and socio-economic approaches in some form, he goes further by suggesting that their importance has been under-emphasised and explores relationships between ideas and (powerful) interests.

The importance of his emphasis on ideas is highlighted here to prompt a discussion on the potential role *academic* ideas may play in tourism policy formation. This should be contrasted with the influence universities may have in policy formation more generally; it is acknowledged that universities can exert influence on local policy-makers as major landowners and employers, and, potentially, play a role in legitimating the power of others (see, for example, Thomas 2010). However, a detailed reading of John's book suggests that academic ideas play little or no part in the main theoretical frameworks that explain policy change. Indeed, the words 'university' and 'universities' do not even feature in the book's index. This is not a deficiency of the index but a reflection of the unimportance ascribed by mainstream theorising on public policy formation to knowledge constructed in universities.

Mellon and Bramwell (2016: 1383) recently set out to counterbalance the lack of, in their words, 'in-depth research on influences encouraging the inclusion of sustainable tourism ideas in specific policy contexts...'. Their explanation of the factors influencing the adoption of this idea, like John's above, does not encompass the work of academics or universities, regardless of their collective output on this topic. The tangentially related literature on 'evidence-based policy' and 'policy learning' (e.g. Lingard 2013) which could also incorporate discussions about the positive contribution academics might make to each (e.g. Connelly et al. 2016) does not reveal such an emphasis.

John (2012) argues that policy domains face a distinct set of conditions that will, in turn, influence policy formation differently. This justifies some consideration of the literature on policy formation in tourism. Those who have sought to explain the evolution of tourism in different contexts barely mention, and in the vast majority of cases do not mention at all, any contribution made by universities. A recent study of the evolution of European tourism policy highlights a variety of influencing agents but not universities (Estol and Font 2016). Studies with similar goals undertaken in Denmark (Halkier 2014), Greece (Pastras and Bramwell 2013), the Philippines (Santa 2015), Portugal and Spain (Garcia 2014), and Vietnam (Truong 2013) also explain policy innovation and change without reference to the contribution of academic research. Indeed, in their account of tourism policy formation in Australia, Airey and Ruhanen (2014: 157) highlighted how marginal universities were to the process:

> Many respondents expressed disappointment at the role of the universities as sources of information with, for example, a tourism representative commenting that "governments to my experience have not drawn much information from universities in a systematic way" (10). An informed observer from a university commented "I think it is difficult to actually interest government policy-makers and industry sector people in scholarly research here" (12) and an informed observer who combines an academic, industry and government background put it straightforwardly as "the one group that I think is almost totally irrelevant in this space are the academics" (11).

Without wishing to labour the point, barriers to innovation in the Polish tourism industry are not explained by the lack of engagement between policy-makers (or other actors) and tourism academics (Najda-Janoszka and Kopera 2014), and improvements in destination competitiveness generally rely on the actions of other actors and powerful influencers (e.g. Dredge 2006; Komppula 2014; Volgger and Pechlaner 2014). The application of frameworks such as actor-network theory (Arnaboldi and Spiller 2011) or, by contrast, regime theory (Thomas and Thomas 2005), to interrogate tourism policy formation and development, distances the influence of tourism academics' work still further.

None of the above should be taken to imply that academics cannot, or even do not, influence policy at all. Clearly, there are instances where their influence and impact might be significant. Saito and Ruhanen (2017), for example, recently argued that universities sometimes demonstrate 'competent power' which is used to support policy-makers via the provision of research services. They provide several illustrations, each of which is highly applied and might have been provided by consultants and/or training providers. Further, Pyo (2011) advocated an approach to creating connections between academic researchers and the knowledge requirements of destination stakeholders. The co-constructed research agendas he highlights as illustration are said to improve the conditions for local innovation (see also Hoarau and Kline 2014; Jacob et al. 2014). Kelliher and Reinl (2011) and Reinl and Kelliher (2014) have also made claims about the value of public sector interventions for the creation of knowledge sharing networks to strengthen the competitiveness of small tourism firms. There are, no doubt, many hidden examples of collaboration and impact.

The central point being made in this chapter, however, is that these instances are rare, sporadic and often the result of funded initiatives that are not sustained once funding ceases (see also Rodríguez et al. 2014; Thomas 2012). Moreover, investigations that set out to explain innovative policy—or policy change in tourism—usually have little or no reason to discuss the work of academics as researchers or as public intellectuals.

Recent (failed) attempts by a loose consortium of universities in the UK with a research capability in tourism suggest that there is little demand for academic engagement among national policy-makers relating to tourism. Organisations such as Visit Britain and Visit England (which are the same organisation but operate under different brands) have a very clear mandate which is principally about attracting overseas visitors to the UK or attracting visitors from different parts of the country to behave as tourists within the country. Their research teams are small, and their work is consumed mainly by survey work to inform official statistics and other specific initiatives. Interviews with key informants (practitioners) indicate that there are overwhelming capacity and funding constraints preventing collaboration on longer-term projects with academics. In addition, well-documented concerns at the incomprehension of many academic papers, of not knowing who to contact for specific expertise and a common policy-distance (a perceived failure to understand the policy-making world) among academic researchers, remain prominent reasons for not working with universities.

This experience appears not to be confined to the UK. The Australian Sustainable Tourism Cooperative Research Centre (STCRC) gained a degree of international prominence in the early 2000s for its progressive attempt to create strong links between academic researchers, policy-makers and other practitioners. Dwyer et al. (2016) provide an assessment of one of the centres that came under the auspices of the STCRC, namely the Centre for Economic Policy (CEP). Their assessment is sanguine, arguing that significant progress was made to advancing policy analysis during its period of existence. The participation of academics in national and international advisory groups, industry networks and think-tanks led to enhanced mutual understanding. Interview data gathered for this book paint a more nuanced picture. As one research professor noted:

> ... the time that it did work was with the Australian Cooperative Research Centre ... it gave you access to industry ... and that worked in a sense that they allowed us access to them to do the research. Whether that research influenced what they did, I'm not sure and I think one of the reasons that the CRC eventually failed was because there was a lack of stakeholder engagement with what the universities were doing.... supporting things they wanted to do and wanted to see, but when the results were coming out, things had moved on. So we were a little bit slower than we should have been perhaps. I would say however, that a lot of the work was still highly relevant to them ... but I think the majority of the work they were given they didn't take away and utilise. Some did but the majority did not. And I'm not quite sure why ... I think that might be the nature of tourism.

It is noteworthy that when the public funding ceased in 2010, the STCRC came to an end. This provides further corroboration of an observation made earlier; pump-priming programmes to demonstrate the potential value of academic research to practitioners do not appear to lead to sustainable self-funding collaboration between industry, policy-makers and academia.

Concluding Comment: The Invisibility of Universities in Explanations of Commercial or Policy Innovation

Academic researchers often narrate their impact by starting with the quality of their research and its value to others. The subsequent claims to impact may involve citations in official documents, consultancy reports or, more recently, indices such as altmetric scores. In the UK, the case for impact has been presented predominantly as an impact case study (for the periodic national performance assessment of subject-based research units) or via multi-annual impact statements for research council funded projects. This chapter's starting point is somewhat different. The initial focus is not on the researcher or the research but on the processes that academics claim to influence. More specifically, it has considered explanations for commercial innovation and for tourism policy change (innovation).

The discussion has shown that flows of knowledge into organisations are an important part of most explanations of innovation. Yet, current theorising and associated empirical studies barely mention academic research as an influential source of knowledge in the context of commercial actors or among policy-makers. Hjalager's (2015) examination of the hundred innovations that transformed tourism provides stark illustration; her paper did not once need to refer to work conducted within or in collaboration with universities. Regardless of the proclamations of research policy, this suggests that the potential for academic research to have a sustained—as opposed to sporadic—impact on the behaviour or decisions of commercial practitioners or policy-makers in tourism and other marginal sectors is very limited indeed.

References

Abreu-Novais, M., Ruhanen, L., & Arcodia, C. (2015). Destination competitiveness: What we know, what we know but shouldn't and what we don't know but should. *Current Issues in Tourism, 19*(6), 492–512.

Airey, D., & Ruhanen, L. (2014). Tourism policy-making in Australia: A national and state perspective. *Tourism Planning and Development, 11*(2), 149–162.

Alsos, G. A., Eide, D., & Madsen, E. L. (Eds.). (2014). *Handbook of research on innovation in tourism industries* (pp. 1–24). Cheltenham: Edward Elgar.

Amabile, T. M. (1997). Motivating creativity in organizations: On doing what you love and loving what you do. *California Management Review, 40*, 39–58.

Amabile, T. M., Conti, R., Coon, H., Lazenby, J., & Herron, M. (1996). Assessing the work environment for creativity. *Academy of Management Journal, 39*(5), 1154–1184.

Anderson, N., Potocnik, K., & Zhou, J. (2014). Innovation and creativity in organisations: A state-of-the-science review, prospective commentary, and guiding framework. *Journal of Management, 40*(5), 1297–1333.

Arnaboldi, M., & Spiller, N. (2011). Actor-network theory and stakeholder collaboration: The case of Cultural Districts. *Tourism Management, 32*(3), 641–654.

Arta, M., & Acob, J. (2003). Innovation in the tourism sector: Results from a pilot study in the Balearic Islands. *Tourism Economics, 9*(3), 279–295.

Autio, E., Kenney, M., Mustar, P., Siegel, D., & Wright, M. (2014). Entrepreneurial innovation: The importance of context. *Research Policy, 43,* 1097–1108.

Baggio, R. & Cooper, C. (2010). Knowledge transfer in a tourism destination: The effect of a network structure. *Service Industries Journal, 30*(10), 1757–1771.

Beamish, G. (2005). How chief executives learn and what behaviour factors distinguish them from other people. *Industrial and Commercial Training, 37*(3), 138–144.

Beesley, L. (2005). The management of emotion in collaborative tourism research settings. *Tourism Management, 26,* 261–275.

Carlisle, S., Kunc, M., Jones, E., & Tiffin, S. (2013). Supporting innovation for tourism development through multi-stakeholder approaches: Experiences from Africa. *Tourism Management, 35,* 59–69.

Chang, S., Gong, Y., Way, S. A., & Jia, L. (2013). Flexibility-oriented HRM systems, absorptive capacity, and market responsiveness and firm innovativeness. *Journal of Management, 39*(7), 1924–1951.

Chen, W.-J. (2011). Innovation in hotel services: Culture and personality. *International Journal of Hospitality Management, 30,* 64–72.

Chesbrough, H. W. (2003). *Open innovation: The new imperative for creating and profiting from technology.* Boston: Harvard Business School Publishing Corporation.

Cohen, W. M., & Levinthal, D. A. (1990). Absorptive capacity: A new perspective on learning and innovation. *Administrative Science Quarterly, 35*(1), 128–152.

Connelly, S., Vanderhoven, D., Durose, C. Richardson, L., Mathews, P., & Rutherford, R. (2016). Translation across borders: Exploring the use, relevance and impact of academic research in the policy process. *After urban regeneration: Communities, policy and place* (pp. 181–198). Bristol: Policy Press.

Cooke, P., Asheim, B., Boschma, R., Martin, R., Schwartz, D., & Tödtling, F. (Eds.). (2011). *Handbook of regional innovation and growth.* Cheltenham: Edward Elgar.

Cooper, C. (2006). Knowledge management and tourism. *Annals of Tourism Research, 33*(1), 47–64.

Cross, R., Parker, A., Prusak, L., & Borgatti, S. P. (2001). Knowing what we know: Supporting knowledge creation and sharing in social networks. *Organisational Dynamics, 30*(2), 100–120.

Czernek, K. (2017). Tourism features as determinants of knowledge transfer in the process of tourist cooperation. *Current Issues in Tourism, 20*(2), 204–220.

Díaz-Chao, Á., Miralbell-Izard, O., & Torrent-Sellens, J. (2016). Information and communication technologies, innovation, and firm productivity in small and medium-sized travel agencies: New evidence from Spain. *Journal of Travel Research, 55*(7), 862–873.

Dredge, D. (2006). Policy networks and the local organisation of tourism. *Tourism Management, 27,* 269–280.

Dwyer, L., & Edwards, D. (2009). Tourism product and service innovation to avoid 'strategic drift'. *International Journal of Tourism Research, 11,* 321–335.

Dwyer, L., Forsyth, P., & Spurr, R. (2016). Tourism economics and policy analysis: Contributions and legacy of the Sustainable Tourism Cooperative Research Centre. *Journal of Hospitality and Tourism Management, 26,* 91–99.

Easterby-Smith, M., Antonacopoulou, E., & Ferdinand, J. (2008). Absorptive capacity: A process perspective. *Management Learning, 39*(5), 483–501.

Estol, J., & Font, X. (2016). European tourism policy: Its evolution and structure. *Tourism Management, 52,* 230–241.

Ford, C. M. (1996). A theory of individual creative action in multiple social domains. *Academy of Management Review, 21,* 1112–1142.

Fosfuri, A., & Tribo, J. A. (2008). Exploring the antecedents of potential absorptive capacity and its impact on innovation performance. *Omega, 36,* 173–187.

Gallego, J., Rubalcaba, L., & Suarez, C. (2013). Knowledge for innovation in Europe: The role of external knowledge on firms' cooperation strategies. *Journal of Business Research, 66*(10), 2034–2041.

Garcia, F. A. (2014). A comparative study of the evolution of tourism policy in Spain and Portugal. *Tourism Management Perspectives, 11,* 34–50.

Garud, R., Gehman, J., & Guiliani, A. P. (2014). Contextualising entrepreneurial innovation: A narrative perspective. *Research Policy, 43,* 1177–1188.

Gunnlaugson, O. (2007). Shedding light on underlying forms of transformative learning theory. *Journal of Transformative Education, 5*(2), 134–151.

Halkier, H. (2014). Innovation and destination governance in Denmark: Tourism, policy networks and spatial development. *European Planning Studies, 22*(8), 1659–1670.

Hall, C. M. (2009). Innovation and tourism policy in Australia and New Zealand: Never the twain shall meet? *Journal of Policy Research in Tourism, Leisure and Events, 1*(1), 2–18.

Hall, C. M. (2011). Publish and perish? Bibliometric analysis, journal ranking and the assessment of research quality in tourism. *Tourism Management, 32*(1), 16–27.

Hall, C. M., & Williams, A. M. (2008). *Tourism and innovation*. London: Routledge.

Hashim, K. F., & Tan, F. B. (2015). The mediating role of trust and commitment on members' continuous knowledge sharing intention: A commitment-trust theory perspective. *International Journal of Information Management, 35,* 145–151.

Hertog, P. M., Gallouj, F., & Segers, J. (2011). Measuring innovation in a 'low tech' service industry: The case of the Dutch hospitality industry. *The Service Industries Journal, 31*(9), 1429–1449.

Hjalager, A.-M. (2002). Repairing innovation defectiveness in tourism. *Tourism Management, 23*(5), 465–474.

Hjalager, A.-M. (2010). A review of innovation research in tourism. *Tourism Management, 31,* 1–12.

Hjalager, A.-M. (2015). 100 innovations that transformed tourism. *Journal of Travel Research, 54*(1), 3–21.

Hjalager, A.-M., & Flagestad, A. (2012). Innovations in well-being tourism in the Nordic countries. *Current Issues in Tourism, 15*(8), 725–740.

Hoarau, H., & Kline, C. (2014). Science and industry: Sharing knowledge for innovation. *Annals of Tourism Research, 46,* 44–61.

Inkpen, A. C., & Tsang, E. W. K. (2005). Social capital, networks and knowledge transfer. *Academy of Management Review, 30*(1), 146–165.

Jacob, M., Florido, C., & Payeras, M. (2014). Knowledge production in two mature destinations. *Annals of Tourism Research, 48,* 280–284.

John, P. (2012). *Analysing public policy* (2nd ed.). London: Routledge.

Kallmuenzer, A., & Peters, M. (2018). Innovativeness and control mechanisms in tourism and hospitality family firms: A comparative study. *International Journal of Hospitality Management, 70,* 66–74.

Kanter, R. M. (1983). *The change masters.* London: Unwin.

Kelliher, F., & Reinl, L. (2011). From facilitated to independent tourism learning networks: Connecting the dots. *Tourism Planning and Development, 8*(2), 185–197.

Kianto, A., Saenz, J., & Aramburu, N. (2017). Knowledge-based human resource management practices, intellectual capital and innovation. *Journal of Business Research, 81,* 11–20.

King, B. E., Breen, J., & Whitelaw, P. A. (2014). Hungry for growth? Small and medium-sized tourism enterprise (SMTE) business ambitions, knowledge acquisition and industry engagement. *International Journal of Tourism Research, 16*(3), 272–281.

Komppula, R. (2014). The role of individual entrepreneurs in the development of competitiveness for a rural tourism destination—A case study. *Tourism Management, 40,* 361–371.

Lane, P. J., Koka, B. R., & Pathak, S. (2006). The reification of absorptive capacity: A critical review and rejuvenation of the construct. *Academy of Management Review, 31*(4), 833–863.

Laursen, K., & Salter, A. J. (2014). The paradox of openness: Appropriability, external search and collaboration. *Research Policy, 43,* 867–878.

Li, Y., Wood, E., & Thomas, R. (2017). Innovation implementation: Harmony and conflict in Chinese modern music festivals. *Tourism Management, 63,* 87–99.

Lingard, B. (2013). The impact of research on education policy in an era of evidence-based policy. *Critical Studies in Education, 54*(2), 113–131.

Lopez-Vega, H., Tell, F., & Vanhaverbeke, W. (2016). Where and how to search? Search paths in open innovation. *Research Policy, 45,* 125–136.

Martinez-Roman, J. A., Tamayo, J. A., Gamero, J., & Romero, J. E. (2015). Innovativeness and business performances in tourism SMEs. *Annals of Tourism Research, 54,* 118–135.

McCabe, V. (2009). 'Butterflying' career patterns in the convention and exhibition industry: A research perspective. In T. Baum, M. Deery, C. Hanlon, L. Lockstone, & K. Smith (Eds.), *People and work in events and conventions* (pp. 51–64). Wallingford: CABI.

Mellon, V., & Bramwell, B. (2016). Protected area policies and sustainable tourism: Influences, relationships and co-evolution. *Journal of Sustainable Tourism, 24*(10), 1369–1386.

Mezirow, J. (1991). *Transformative dimensions of adult learning.* San Francisco: Josey-Bass Publishers.

Mezirow, J. (2000). Learning to think like an adult: Core concepts of transformation theory. In J. Mezirow (Ed.), *Learning as transformation: Critical perspectives on a theory in progress* (pp. 3–33). San Francisco: Jossey-Bass.

Mezirow, J. (2003). Transformative learning as discourse. *Journal of Transformative Education, 1*(1), 58–63.

Mezirow, J. (2009). Transformative learning theory. In J. Mezirow & W. Taylor (Eds.), *Transformative learning in practice: Insights from community, workplace and higher education* (pp. 18–32). San Francisco: Jossey-Bass.

Mina, A., Bascavusoglu-Moreau, E., & Hughes, A. (2014). Open service innovation and the firm's search for external knowledge. *Research Policy, 43,* 853–866.

Moon, J. J. A. (2002). *Reflection in learning and professional development: Theory and practice.* London: Kogan Page.

Najda-Janoszka, M., & Kopera, S. (2014). Exploring barriers to innovation in tourism industry—The case of southern region of Poland. *Procedia—Social and Behavioural Sciences, 110,* 190–201.

Nieves, J., & Segarra-Cipres, M. (2015). Management innovation in the hotel industry. *Tourism Management, 46,* 51–58.

Orfila-Sintes, F., Crespi-Cladera, R., & Martinez-Ros, E. (2005). Innovation activity in the hotel industry: Evidence from the Balearic Islands. *Tourism Management, 26,* 851–865.

Ottenbacher, M. C. (2007). Innovation management in the hospitality industry: Different strategies for achieving success. *Journal of Hospitality and Tourism Research, 31*(4), 431–454.

Pastras, P., & Bramwell, B. (2013). A strategic-relational approach to tourism policy. *Annals of Tourism Research, 43,* 390–414.

Pittaway, L., Robertson, M., Munir, K., Denyer, D., & Neely, N. (2004). *Networking and innovation in the UK: A systematic review of the literature.* London: AIM.

Presenza, A., & Cipollina, M. (2010). Analysing tourism stakeholder networks. *Tourism Review., 65*(4), 17–30.

Pyo, S. (2011). Identifying and prioritizing destination knowledge needs. *Annals of Tourism Research, 39*(2), 1156–1175.

Reinl, L., & Kelliher, F. (2010). Cooperative micro-firm strategies: Leveraging resources through learning networks. *International Journal of Entrepreneurship and Innovation, 11*(2), 141–150.

Reinl, L., & Kelliher, F. (2014). The social dynamics of micro-firm learning in an evolving learning community. *Tourism Management, 40,* 117–125.

Ritala, P., Olander, H., Michailova, S., & Husted, K. (2015). Knowledge sharing, knowledge leaking and relative innovation performance: An empirical study. *Technovation, 35,* 22–31.

Rodríguez, I., Williams, A. M., & Hall, C. M. (2014). Tourism innovation policy: Implementation and outcomes. *Annals of Tourism Research, 49,* 76–93.

Rogers, T. (2013). *Conferences and conventions: A global industry.* London: Routledge.

Ryu, H.-S., & Lee, J.-N. (2016). Innovation patterns and their effects on firm performance. *Service Industries Journal, 36*(3–4), 81–101.

Saito, H., & Ruhanen, L. (2017). Power in tourism stakeholder collaborations: Power types and power holders. *Journal of Hospitality and Tourism Management, 31,* 189–196.

Santa, E. D. (2015). The Evolution of Philippine Tourism Policy Implementation from 1973 to 2009. *Tourism Planning and Development, 12*(2), 155–175.

Scott, N., & Ding, P. (2008). Management of tourism research knowledge in Australia and China. *Current Issues in Tourism, 11*(6), 514–528.

Scott, N., Baggio, R., & Cooper, C. (2008). *Network analysis and tourism: From theory to practice.* Clevedon: Channel View Publications.

Shaw, G. (2015). Tourism networks, knowledge dynamics and co-creation. In M. McLeod & R. Vaughan (Eds.), *Knowledge networks and tourism* (pp. 45–61). London: Routledge.

Shaw, G., & Williams, A. (2009). Knowledge transfer and management in tourism organisations: An emerging research agenda. *Tourism Management, 30*(3), 325–335.

Sherlock, J. J., & Nathan, M. L. (2008). How power dynamics impact the content and process of nonprofit CEO learning. *Management Learning, 39*(3), 245–269.

Smith, M., Busi, N., Ball, P., & Van der Meer, R. (2008). Factors influencing an organisation's ability to manage innovation: A structured literature review and conceptual model. *International Journal of Innovation Management, 12*(4), 655–676.

Sorensen, F. (2007). The geographies of social networks and innovation in tourism. *Tourism Geographies, 9*(1), 22–48.

Stahl, G. K., Maznevski, M. L., Voigt, A., & Jonsen, K. (2009). Unravelling the effects of cultural diversity in teams: A meta-analysis of research on multicultural work groups. *Journal of International Business Studies, 41*, 690–709.

Tejada, P., & Moreno, P. (2013). Patterns of innovation in tourism 'small and medium sized enterprises'. *The Service Industries Journal, 33*(7–8), 749–758.

Thomas, H. (2010). Knowing the city: Local coalitions, knowledge and research. In C. Allen & R. Imrie (Eds.), *The knowledge business* (pp. 77–92). Farnham: Ashgate.

Thomas, R. (2007). Tourism partnerships and small firms: Power, participation and partition. *International Journal of Entrepreneurship and Innovation, 8*(1), 37–44.

Thomas, R. (2012). Business elites, universities and knowledge transfer in tourism. *Tourism Management, 33*(3), 553–561.

Thomas, R., & Thomas, H. (2005). Understanding tourism policy-making in urban areas, with particular reference to small firms. *Tourism Geographies, 7*(2), 121–137.

Thomas, R., & Wood, E. (2014). Innovation in tourism: Re-conceptualising and measuring the absorptive capacity of the hotel sector. *Tourism Management, 45*, 39–48.

Thomas, R., & Wood, E. (2015). The absorptive capacity of tourism organisations. *Annals of Tourism Research, 54*, 84–99.

Thomas, R., Shaw, G., & Page, S. J. (2011). Understanding small firms in tourism: A perspective on research trends and challenges. *Tourism Management, 32*(5), 963–976.

Truong, V. D. (2013). Tourism policy development in Vietnam: A pro-poor perspective. *Journal of Policy Research in Tourism, Leisure and Events, 5*(1), 28–45.

Unsworth, K. L., & Clegg, C. W. (2010). Why do employees undertake creative action? *Journal of Occupational and Organizational Psychology, 83*, 77–99.

Van de Ven, A. H., Polley, D. E., Garud, R., & Venkataraman, S. (2008). *The innovation journey.* Oxford: Oxford University Press.

Vega-Jurado, J., Gutierrez-Garcia, A., Fernandez-de-Lucio, I., & Manjarres-Henriquez, L. (2008). Analysing the determinants of a firm's absorptive capacity: Beyond R&D. *R&D Management, 38*(4), 392–405.

Vega-Jurado, J., Gutierrez-Garcia, A., & Fernandez-de-Lucio, I. (2009). Does external knowledge sourcing matter for innovation? Evidence from the Spanish manufacturing industry. *Industrial and Corporate Change, 18*(4), 637–670.

Volgger, M., & Pechlaner, H. (2014). Requirements for destination management organizations in destination governance: Understanding DMO success. *Tourism Management, 41*, 64–75.

Wang, M.-C., Chen, P.-C., & Fang, S.-C. (2018). A critical view of knowledge networks and innovation performance: The mediation role of firms' knowledge integration capability. *Journal of Business Research, 88*, 222–233.

Weber, K., & Ladkin, A. (2009). Career anchors of convention and exhibition industry professionals in Asia. *Journal of Convention and Event Tourism, 10*, 243–255.

Weidenfeld, A., Williams, A. M., & Butler, R. W. (2010). Knowledge transfer and innovation among attractions. *Annals of Tourism Research, 37*(3), 604–626.

West, J., Salter, A., Vanhaverbeke, W., & Chesbrough, H. (2014). Open innovation: The next decade. *Research Policy, 43*, 805–811.

Williams, A. M., & Shaw, G. (2011). Internationalization and innovation in tourism. *Annals of Tourism Research, 38*(1), 27–51.

Xiao, H., & Smith, S. L. J. (2006). The use of tourism knowledge: Research propositions. *Annals of Tourism Research, 34*(2), 310–331.

Xiao, H., & Smith, S. L. J. (2007). The use of tourism knowledge: Research propositions. *Annals of Tourism Research, 34*(2), 310–331.

Xiao, H., & Smith, S. L. J. (2009). Knowledge impact: An appraisal of tourism scholarship. *Annals of Tourism Research, 35*(1), 62–83.

Zach, F. J., & Hill, T. L. (2017). Network, knowledge and relationship impacts on innovation in tourism destinations. *Tourism Management, 62*, 196–207.

Zahra, S. A., & George, G. (2002). Absorptive capacity: A review, reconceptualization, and extension. *Academy of Management Review, 27*(2), 185–203.

Zheng, Y., & Yang, H. (2015). Does familiarity foster innovation? The impact of alliance partner repeatedness on breakthrough innovations. *Journal of Management Studies, 52*(2), 213–230.

Zhou, J., & Shalley, C. E. (2010). Deepening our understanding of creativity in the workplace: A review of different approaches to creativity research. In S. Zedeck (Ed.), *APA Handbook of Industrial and Organizational Psychology* (Vol. 1, pp. 275–302). Washington, DC: American Psychological Association.

CHAPTER 3

Professional Associations as Conduits of Knowledge: Ethnographic Reflections

I tend to mix with people at the peer group sort of level. I use the (name of association) for that (acquiring knowledge).
Senior practitioner interviewed for ESRC funded research on knowledge acquisition among business elites

Abstract Professional associations are often considered to be valuable conduits for knowledge exchange between practitioners and universities. Their advocacy of professional standards, continuous professional development and 'best practice' resonate comfortably with statements universities make about research impact. This chapter draws upon research into the professionalisation of occupations in tourism and events (Thomas and Thomas in Tourism Manage Perspect 6:8–14, 2013; Thomas and Thomas in Serv Ind J 34:38–55, 2014) and reports ethnographic reflections on *pro bono* and paid work undertaken by the author with the Institute of Travel and Tourism (ITT) and the Association of British Professional Conference Organisers (ABPCO). It argues that collaborative activity does not represent a stimulus for the promotion and utilisation of research insights for more effective practice (impact) but a benign harnessing of academic work to create stories for their members.

Keywords Tourism studies · Universities · Theory-practice gap

© The Author(s) 2018   47
R. Thomas, *Questioning the Assessment of Research Impact*, Palgrave Critical University Studies,
https://doi.org/10.1007/978-3-319-95723-4_3

Introduction

A recent tribute to Victor Middleton, one of the first prominent British tourism scholars, noted that 'When he was a full time academic he always effectively linked his work and his publications to the practice and management of tourism' (Airey 2016: 6). It appears that his efforts to engage practitioners was rendered a success by his consistently 'bridging theory and practice in tourism'. This assessment is informed, quite reasonably, by the testimony of several influential industry leaders and public policy-makers, and by linking Middleton's 'practical' achievements with his outputs as a researcher, implying that the latter informed the former or that they were at least connected in some way (see also Lamoureux 2017).

Certainly, few would argue that Middleton's career was anything other than illustrious. It was peppered with honours and awards, all of which confirmed his status as one of the sector's luminaries. His academic profile was probably fuelled most by the popularity of his textbooks and because of his championing of tourism as a subject for study in universities. The pivotal role he played in setting up what became the Tourism Society and the projects he led as a consultant raised his profile among practitioners. His subsequent attempts at forging connections between universities and practitioners via the Society prompt important questions about the potentially valuable mediating role that professional associations may play in an exchange of knowledge between academics and practitioners.

This chapter provides ethnographic reflections on my more modest efforts to perform a similar 'bridging' function between universities and, as separate projects, the Institute of Travel and Tourism (ITT) and the Association of British Professional Conference Organisers (ABPCO). The forms of collaboration are documented and their implications for knowledge exchange and innovation are assessed. Prior to that, a brief review of professionalisation in the context of tourism is required.

Attempts at professionalising tourism, in the classic sense of the term, have failed in the UK (Thomas and Thomas 2014). Perhaps the most common, though arguably flawed, way of assessing the extent to which occupations have become professionalised uses a theoretical vantage point often called the traits approach. In essence, the characteristics of occupations which are widely regarded as having been professionalised, notably medicine and law, are listed and then compared with the occupation being studied. Sheldon (1989), an early advocate, created a list of twelve traits based on her review of the literature. Her suggestion was that professionalised occupations require, *inter alia*, practitioners to undergo an extensive training and education, to understand a defined body of knowledge, to subscribe to a code of ethics and to be a member of an association that is governed independently by its members (see also Haywood-Farmer and Stuart 1990; McNamee et al. 2000). The resulting social contract holds that a professionalised occupation has prestige and is well paid, in the knowledge that practitioners will act ethically and safeguard the public interest.

Burgess (2011) used the traits approach to examine the professionalisation of hotel management. As she stated:

> (the aim) is to consider whether the traits that define a professional can be applied in hotels... (the findings of) a recent research project will be used to determine whether the traits can be applied...and hence whether they can be considered as a profession. (Burgess 2011: 682)

Her conclusion was that hotel management could not be considered a professionalised occupation because the subjects of her study did not display the requisite characteristics. The professional association to which the managers belonged was too 'open', did not insist on professional updating and was of little appeal to many employers or to prospective members. There was, in the language of the professionalisation literature, no occupational closure (Thomas and Thomas 2014).

Formadi and Raffai (2009) adopt the traits approach for their assessment of event management in Hungary and argue that there is an emerging professionalisation to the extent that 'the events management sector...is being recognized throughout the country as a professional field... (and) the prestige of the field is growing' (Formadi and Raffai 2009: 88–89). In a departure from others, they emphasise one trait in particular, namely the role of specialist knowledge relating to such matters such as public safety and crowd dynamics. Harris (2004) is equally sanguine in her assessment of British event management, though she fails to provide any empirical evidence to support her case or to counter the observation that membership levels of associations are almost imperceptible in the UK and relatively small elsewhere in the world (Thomas and Thomas 2013).

Sociological studies of 'modern' occupations tend to theorise professionalisation in different terms. Rather than emphasising empirically undemonstrated traits and perhaps legitimising further the potentially self-serving self-images promoted by 'professions' (Thomas 1991: 35), much recent theorising has concentrated on what is often termed 'corporate professionalisation' (see, for example, Muzio et al. 2011; Muzio and Kirkpatrick 2011). Thomas and Thomas (2014) argue that such an approach appears more suitable for tourism:

> It offers a valuable lens to examine developments within tourism; a non-statutory policy domain in the UK that has emphasised partnership with the private sector and, although it remains characterised by small firms, has also experienced trends towards concentration in at least some subsectors, notably travel. (Thomas and Thomas 2014: 43)

Although perspectives vary, one of the distinguishing features of corporate professionalisation is the emphasis it places on commercialism as opposed to public service—on the 'added value' of using professionals as opposed to safeguards to welfare. This is an appropriate conceptualisation in an age when most 'professionals' work within private companies. As Muzio et al. (2011: 458) explain:

> Accordingly, the reference point here is no longer an increasingly neoliberal and budget-conscious state .... (that) is sceptical of professional claims and practices, but the market .... In other words, these associations set out to build a critical mass of consensus around their project and activities by persuading a sufficiently large number of employing organisations and consumers of the commercial merits and safeguards associated with professional membership, accreditation and regulation. The idea being that once a sufficiently large share of the market has been won over and professional qualifications become embedded in corporate tendering processes, professional affiliation would be routinely expected and indeed requested by both clients and employers in their procurement and recruitment strategies; thus, de facto, delivering a market form of occupational closure.

In this context, professionalism becomes a resource; it allows occupations to present themselves positively to advance their commercial interests (Kipping 2011). Thus, the claims to legitimacy made by professional associations tend to emphasise the commercial benefits that accrue to those using the services of their members. These arise, *inter alia*, from their ability to use cutting-edge techniques or practices promoted by the association to gain competitive advantage. It is common, therefore, for associations to speak of their role as facilitators of 'best practice', providers of 'thought leadership' and advocates for 'evidence-based decision-making'.

It is not surprising that professional associations are often seen as important conduits for knowledge. One of the challenges they face, however, is how to overcome a fragmented, often client or context specific, knowledge base as a means of moving towards what might be represented as a coherent body of knowledge. This challenge applies equally to identifying best practice. Arguably, universities may play a useful role in this respect by helping to consolidate knowledge and by identifying, via their research, the most effective practices. Muzio and Kirkpatrick (2011) provide evidence that illustrates this potential by reference to the museums sector. Their research shows how service delivery models were developed in the USA by the professional association and that this had the effect of changing museum design and employment practices.

In the British tourism and events sectors, professional associations typically share best practice and provide opportunities for members to learn via a battery of local, national and international networking events. The associations' business models are such that many events are free, perhaps in a venue hosted by a member, while others involve a substantial charge because they use celebrity headline speakers and take place in five-star resort hotels. Inevitably, each type of event attracts a different constituency. Few of the events have, historically, included a contribution from academics or the reporting of their research. This is, perhaps, predicatble in light of the discussion on knowledge flows presented in Chapter 2.

The next section discusses the approaches to creating knowledge flows from universities to practitioners adopted by the Institute of Travel and Tourism (ITT) and the Association of British Professional Conference Organisers (ABPCO). It does so as part of an assessment of the potential for research impact arising from working with professional associations.

THE INSTITUTE OF TRAVEL AND TOURISM (ITT)

Between 2007 and 2011, I was the ITT Professor of Tourism and Events Policy at the then Leeds Metropolitan (now Leeds Beckett) University, UK. The arrangement resulted in my providing a range of services to the Institute in exchange for financial and non-financial consideration. The formal partnership between the association and my employer came about as a result of research work that brought me into contact with senior members of tourism professional associations. The project that subsequently became Thomas and Thomas (2014) started in 2006. As part of the data gathering process, I interviewed senior members of the ITT and other organisations that defined themselves in similar terms. By coincidence, those leading the association were reviewing its direction and were seeking ways of showing members that it did more than organise networking events. It had recently emerged from a somewhat precarious financial position and was seeking new initiatives as it entered a period of greater stability and growth. There is a degree of consensus that the change in its fortunes was the result of a successful blend of prudence and the entrepreneurial flair of the Chief Executive and Chair (the same person).

One of the distinctive aspects of the ITT is its orientation towards the commercial sector and, more specifically, those that work in 'travel' (tour operators, travel agents and associated suppliers) rather than practitioners and policy-makers interested in inbound tourism. An audit of current and past Board members and attendees at ITT events provides confirmatory evidence of this. Indeed, it is interesting that the title Institute of Travel would probably convey its orientation more accurately. However, as part of its failed attempt to stymie the formation of the Tourism Society in the early 1970s, it added 'tourism' to its title (Thomas and Thomas 2014) leading some to slightly misleading conclusions about its remit and area of interest.

My appointment was announced as a front page 'splash' in the ITT's newsletter and the trade press also took an interest, particularly Travel Weekly who was the ITT's 'media partner' (www.travelweekly.co.uk/articles/23319/university-joins-institute-of-travel-and-tourism-board-11-jan-2007). The opening line of the former stated that 'In a unique alliance between the travel industry and the academic world, Professor Rhodri Thomas of Leeds Metropolitan University has been appointed as ITT's first university Chair. The industry has never before worked so closely with an academic institution … ITT is the first travel association to appoint an academic Chair'.

My inaugural lecture for the association was at its international conference in Gran Canaria in June 2007. Remarkably, I shared a billing in the promotional literature with illustrious speakers such as Manny Fontenla-Novoa, then Chief Executive Officer of Thomas Cook plc, the author

Bill Bryson, and the Rt. Honourable Charles Kennedy MP, then Leader of the Liberal Democrats (though illness prevented his attendance). I was the first tourism academic to have been given an opportunity to address the movers and shakers of this sector via this annual flagship event. Clearly, being able to weave this kind of incident into a narrative about university engagement and using the development of this kind of network to strengthen stories of academic impact on practitioners were seen by many colleagues as highly desirable.

The focus of the lecture was the professionalisation of travel and tourism. In an attempt to demonstrate that I was worthy of the title 'ITT Professor', I sought to provide an analysis that was well informed, drawing on data gathered specifically for the event, and offered practical policy recommendations for the association. Reflecting the academic literature discussed above, I argued that if the sector were to be professionalised, the prominence of the Institute needed to be enhanced. Experience from other sectors suggested that professionalised occupations had institutes that were persuasive; they had managed to persuade sufficient numbers of potential members to join (i.e. enough had been convinced that there were benefits to be gained from joining) and had persuaded employers that recruiting members of the professional association would yield them high calibre staff. At the time of the lecture, recognition rates among undergraduates were low and few employers, if any (none could be identified), were asking for membership of the ITT as a preferred 'qualification' for the job. The lecture was received politely by delegates and generated a degree of interest in the trade press (e.g. www.travelweekly.co.uk/articles/24403/industry-short-on-quality-says-tourism-professor-31-may-2007 and www.travelweekly.co.uk/articles/24497/itt-lack-of-professionalism-in-industry-deterring-graduates-8-jUNE-2007). This was a theme I returned to in subsequent years but it did not stimulate a significant change of strategy.

Constitutionally, the Board was the key decision-making body of the organisation. My impression was that the charismatic Chair and a small group of long-standing elected Board members were disproportionately influential. The Board made or ratified decisions relating to finance and held the Chair (who was also the Chief Executive Officer) to account. For the period of my involvement, Board members included very senior staff from highly prominent businesses, often functional directors or CEOs, and others with more modest employment histories. That remains the case (www.itt.co.uk).

The secretariat of the association was, and continues to be, sub-contracted to an events agency. This is consistent with the emphasis placed by the Institute on providing events which afford opportunities for peer-to-peer learning. These were seen as being popular with members because they allowed for the development of social and professional networks.

The evident pride taken in the events programme is understandable given the profile of powerful speakers that they are able to attract. While some 'circuit' speakers (well-known authors, entertainers or sports people who, for example, give pep talks on teamwork or the importance of coaching) appear on the programmes, most time is devoted to creating opportunities to learn from the experiences of CEOs of large companies (from Tesco plc to Thomas Cook plc) or former ministers (e.g. former Chancellor George Osborne) and other senior politicians.

Immediately prior to my relationship with the ITT, there was no academic representation on ITT's Board and only one (semi-)active member on the Education and Training Committee worked in a university. The organisation had little experience of working with universities; many Board members were not graduates themselves and few had any appreciation of the research undertaken by academics. Perhaps not surprisingly, reactions to the greater involvement of academics, personified by me during the early stages of what became a project to strengthen collaborative links, ranged from the evident enthusiasm of the Chair to indifference, scepticism and, even, discomfort.

The purpose and orientation of the Education and Training Committee during the early stages of my involvement appeared to me to be unclear and conservative. Although its activities were reported to the Board, it enjoyed little autonomy that involved expenditure (there was no separate budget, for example) and it exerted little organisational influence. Even on matters that might be seen as central to its remit, such as my role, it did not have a voice and was not involved in my appointment. I negotiated my work with the Chair and reported to him and the Board, though I also attended Education and Training Committee meetings. Perhaps my most surprising realisation was the lack of a coherent perspective on how the Committee might influence education and training in the UK at various levels and how this might, in turn, contribute to the professionalisation of the occupation (however that might be defined). Perhaps my involvement was seen as compensating for this.

The lack of active academic membership of the ITT was probably because the association did not have a presence in the consciousness of academics or students. The first report in what was to become a series of three ITT research reports provided evidence to confirm anecdotal presumptions about the very low levels of student recognition of professional associations in the sector. The survey of almost 1000 tourism undergraduates suggested that fewer than two per cent of the students could name associations, even when given acronyms (Thomas 2007). Anecdotal evidence from the time suggests that similar figures would probably have applied to academic members of staff; this makes it less surprising that their students had not heard of, let alone joined, associations which claimed to be at the vanguard of professionalising the sector.

The informal strategy agreed with the Chair and Board involved me developing a set of activities that would make the Institute more appealing to potential academic members (and students) and to provide examples of research that could be used by association members to inform their practice. For the former, a package of 'offers' was created, which was designed to interest those who were research active. They included enabling access to senior managers or companies for research purposes and providing channels of communication for disseminating their work to practitioners. In addition, a suite of awards was introduced, encompassing Ph.D. students, which were presented at a prestigious ceremony held at the Houses of Parliament. This was, again, intended to signal the ITT's appreciation of academic research and reflective of its commitment to the industry–academia nexus. The judging panel for the Ph.D. award consisted of senior academics with significant research track records and experience of supervising and examining Ph.D.'s (up to three professors), as well as the Chair of the Institute and the Chair of the Education and Training Committee. The credibility of the awards in the eyes of British academics was important if the initiative was to enhance, rather than diminish, the reputation of the ITT. Securing nominations for the award was challenging initially but the awards flourished once they became known more widely. Prize winners included students from the universities of Newcastle, Nottingham, Strathclyde and Surrey. It is interesting to note in passing that although the awards have been sustained in the intervening period, the judging panel has changed to become members of the Education and Training Committee; they are now, therefore, judged by a panel with little or no research or Ph.D. supervisory experience. One can only speculate about how the awards are perceived by academics nowadays.

In an attempt to gain most value from my engagement with the Institute, and to add academic respectability to the collaborative work being undertaken with them, I applied to the Economic and Social Research Council (ESRC) for funding (grant reference: RES-186-27-0015) to research knowledge acquisition and utilisation among 'business elites'. The term 'business elites' was used to indicate a constituency of individuals who held very senior management roles within large travel and tourism businesses (employing, in some cases, tens of thousands of employees). Understanding more about how they acquired and used knowledge, and their dispositions to the kind of knowledge produced by universities, would enable policy-makers and those working within universities to refine their approaches to engaging such actors. My involvement with the ITT, and their ability to secure the support of a relatively small and inaccessible, yet sectorially influential, group of practitioners, no doubt helped persuade the funders of the novelty and value of the research.

The findings are reported in Thomas (2012) (but see also Thomas 2013). Influenced by Mezirow's (2000, 2009) theorising, the study concluded that transformational learners were open to the breadth of knowledge produced by universities but that, on the whole, there were few in senior positions within large travel companies. Thus, even with novel forms of dissemination, it is unlikely that the formal knowledge that emerges from tourism departments will yield much reassessment of practice among this constituency of managers.

The final aspect of the approach to attracting academics to working with the ITT was to secure follow-on funding from the ESRC (RES-189-25-0205). Follow-on funding is provided by the Council to enhance the impact of the research on non-academic audiences. The grant funded several round-table events which brought senior research-active academics and senior practitioners together for round-table events to explore the value of specific academic research projects. The grant also funded an event for academics where insights from the research and the round-table events could be shared with colleagues and their implications considered.

The round-table events were able to attract senior practitioners because of the active participation of the ITT. Indeed, I am under no illusions that the Managing Directors and Chief Executive Officers who attended did so to support the ITT and its Chair, even though I developed a good independent relationship with several. Equally, the academics were probably easier to persuade because the event was organised under the auspices of the ESRC, though, again, I enjoyed good relationships with many of those making presentations.

The purpose of each event was to showcase good quality academic research on the basis that this might alert influential practitioners to the kinds of outputs produced by the sector and, therefore, 'open minds' or challenge prejudices. Presenters were selected carefully on the basis that they were evidently credible, had current research work that was—*prima facie* at least—of relevance and were able to engage with a senior practitioner audience. The events provided them with a rare opportunity to discuss their work with very senior practitioners, to gain greater understanding of their 'world' and to strengthen their networks with a view to creating additional accounts of impact. The selection of participants took place in close collaboration with the Chair of the ITT and relied upon a high level of shared understanding and mutual trust.

The first round-table event brought together scholars from the universities of Cambridge, Cardiff, Exeter and Leeds with very senior practitioners from the Airport Operators Association, Carnival UK, Eurostar, Flybe, Tui Travel plc, TTA/Worldchoice (www.itt.co.uk/events/events_detail.php?date=2009-09-30) to explore issues associated with climate change and its implications for travel and tourism. The second focused on innovation research funded by the ESRC and undertaken by colleagues from the universities of Exeter and Surrey. I also presented aspects of the research on how business elites learn, as a way of prompting discussion on their openness to external sources of knowledge. This was attended by Director-level personnel from Tui plc, World Travel Market, P&O Ferries, Hilton Hotels and Resorts, and TripAdvisor. The third event returned to climate change as a theme of mutual interest between academics from the following universities: Leeds Metropolitan, Oxford Brookes and Surrey. They were in discussion with senior practitioners from Tui Travel plc, Cooperative Travel and Best Loved Hotels. All were reported in the trade press as well as in ITT newsletters. Stephen Freudmann, Chair of the ITT, was reported in a newsletter as follows: 'The more I participate in activities that bridge the gap between industry and academics, the more convinced I am of their value. We need to try to build on what has been achieved so far' (ITT Bullittin, Spring, 2011).

With the exception of the final event, where some of the speakers were not reporting contemporary research, all round-tables were highly successful. They stimulated interesting discussion and were conducted in a mutually respectful manner with the intention of exchanging (rather than transferring) knowledge, i.e. there was learning on both 'sides'. Informal feedback to the Chair, with some very slight exceptions, was very positive indeed. The initiative was seen as worth supporting ('we should do more of these') and concerns expressed that the momentum should not be lost. Yet, little occurred once the funding ceased and the favours to the ITT, in the form of taking time out of busy offices, had been made. There were no follow-up meetings, no extensions to networks and little or no additional collaboration. Moreover, had there been resources available to promote future events, it would have been challenging to sustain a full programme because of the difficulty involved in identifying enough British academic tourism research that would resonate with commercial managers of the kind that participated in the round-table events. In my experience, this highly significant limiting factor is rarely acknowledged by tourism academics in the UK.

The follow-on funding also enabled me to assess the feasibility of developing a co-created MBA or DBA and to draft a strategy for the ITT aimed at promoting greater knowledge exchange between universities and industry. Both involved speaking with senior practitioners as well as discussions with the ITT's Board. In addition, a breakfast meeting for delegates attending the Institute's 2011 international conference in Venice, Italy, was hosted to garner additional perspectives. For a variety of reasons, a co-created MBA was not considered to be a feasible proposition. These included issues related to the composition of the workforce, perceptions of the knowledge base of tourism academics in the UK and the capability and capacity of the ITT to contribute senior-level managers capable of contributing to programme design and delivery at masters level. A strategy for knowledge exchange was agreed formally by the Board but it resulted in little reassessment of practices. I was left with the sense that it was something of a perfunctory exercise—a requirement to complete the terms of ESRC funding rather than an opportunity to effect change across the sector.

The enabling mechanisms to promote academic research that were likely to be of value to businesses, in addition to the events, included developing web pages and populating them with 'research nuggets' and producing bespoke research reports. The former consisted of summaries of contemporary research published in leading peer-reviewed academic journals. In order not to breach copyright, links were posted online so that members could then click through and purchase the full articles if desired. At the time of writing (March 2018), the original 'nuggets' were still available (http://www.itt.co.uk/careers/research_nuggets. php) and cover topics such as the effectiveness of cabin crew training for managing disruptive airline passengers (Rhoden et al. 2008), a review of research on the factors influencing online travel buying decisions (Wen 2009), research on the key drivers of airline loyalty (Dolnicar et al. 2011) and transport in a climate-constrained world (Schafer et al. 2009). Nothing new has been added to the original postings.

It is somewhat predictable, with the benefit of hindsight, that barely any members used the 'research nuggets'; the web metrics showing usage data were negligble. This was in spite of regular promotion via one of the association's various types of newsletter. Speculation about the reasons for this included members' lack of awareness, the still-academic style of communication and the need for capacity and capability building to show how the research might lead to better decision-making and innovation. As Chapter 2 revealed, the reasons are potentially more complex than this.

A similar fate befell the ITT Research Report Series (see Thomas 2007, 2008, 2009). The topics were prompted by discussions between active members of the Institute and me, and were promoted via newsletters. Some also generated coverage in the trade press (e.g. www. travelweekly.co.uk/articles/30208/flexible-working-more-important-than-ever-says-itt; www.travelweekly.co.uk/articles/28091/travel-trade-out-of-step-on-climate-change-study-finds; www.travelweekly. co.uk/articles/28091/travel-trade-out-of-step-on-climate-change-study-finds) which was seen as making the venture worthwhile. That so few were downloaded and that there was no evidence of new practices being promoted was of little concern. This suggests, again, that the Institute's desire for academic engagement was tied less to notions of providing members with knowledge that would influence the thinking of practitioners but a more mundane, and benign, concern to be seen as dynamic. Actual impact, which was never monitored, mattered less than creating stories to keep the ITT in the public eye.

The ITT did not have regular, or for that matter even periodic, discussions about how to professionalise the sector. Not surprisingly, therefore, there was no coherent formal (or informal) strategy during this period to professionalise tourism that guided their actions. Indeed, it is interesting that at some point during its history, the language of those leading the association changed; it became an 'association of professionals' rather than a professional association in the classic sense of the term. It was almost as though the mission to be a professional association, and all that implied, was lost. This is not a criticism. The ITT produced valuable events for its members and created potentially significant peer-to-peer learning opportunities. It also acted as a very effective conduit for those seeking to develop or nurture their professional network.

The unprecedented collaborative approach discussed in this chapter did not lead to substantial research impact. In spite of the ITT's best efforts, they could not sustain the interest of their members (or, in reality, their Board) in academic research that related to strategic and operational practices. This extended even to those who had enjoyed positive experiences at the round-table events.

Of equal importance to the thesis advanced in this book is the observation that universities could not showcase enough high-quality research that was of interest or relevance to practitioners. The limited availability of 'engaged scholars' (Van de Ven 2007) acts as a significant barrier to sustained engagement and, perhaps subsequently, research impact. Critics might argue that the period discussed revealed the deficiencies of those leading the 'project', notably me. Even allowing for this, the limited lifespan of each initiative suggests that the most progressive professional associations in this sector cannot sustain activities that may be construed as research impact. Instead, they focus on 'creating stories' for their members; it is important to be an interesting and dynamic association that is worthy of its subscription. Association membership creates social and professional networks, which might enable knowledge flows, but does not act as conduit of knowledge from universities beyond externally funded projects. The 'hollowed out' notion of professionalism in tourism (Thomas and Thomas 2014) limits the likelihood of research impact emerging from this source, even in the medium to long term.

THE ASSOCIATION OF BRITISH PROFESSIONAL CONFERENCE ORGANISERS (ABPCO)

The Association of British Professional Conference Organisers (ABPCO) is one of a handful of professional associations that operate in the British events sector. Its almost exclusive focus on association events marks out a territory that separates it from other competing organisations, notably Meeting Professionals International (MPI) and the International Special

Events Society (ISES) (now the International Live Events Association), both of which originate from the USA. It also distinguishes it from the fledgling Institute of Event Management (IEM) which is seeking to become the main professional association for event managers of any kind (for an assessment of its prospects, see Thomas and Thomas 2013).

Although there are similarities between the approaches to professionalisation pursued by the ITT and ABPCO, it would be easy to exaggerate them. Perhaps the most obvious difference is one of scale. The ITT's international conference, for example, is capped at 400 delegates, whereas ABPCO's Chair's annual awards attract approximately 100. Further, the average level of formal education (highest qualification) is different with active ITT members enjoying generally lower levels of attainment than those held by active ABPCO members. The ITT is firmly focused on the commercial priority of selling holidays, whereas the events managed by ABPCO members are more complex and often involve an educational or social aim (such as sharing the latest scientific advances relating to Alzheimer's disease or promoting particular kinds of care). Finally, there are significantly different gender profiles, with predominantly females managing ABPCO. Thus, to read off the analysis of the ITT as if it applied to ABPCO would be misleading.

Nevertheless, in similar fashion to the ITT, ABPCO suffered the vicissitudes of changing membership rates over decades and the negative consequences that follow. It has, however, now established a pattern of activities that has secured a membership base large enough, if still modest, to plan with greater security. A part-time Association Director leads the association with an elected Executive Committee (Board of Directors), of which I was a co-opted member until early 2017.

As its website states:

ABPCO's mission is to develop and enhance the professional status of conference and event organisers and increase the recognition given to its members and to ABPCO as the leading representative of the profession in the British Isles. (www.abpco.org/about-abpco/)

Pursuant to this mission, the association has strategic aims that are operationalised in the form of 'pillars' or priorities. It is noteworthy that between 2015 and 2016, one of these was to 'partner with universities to source and disseminate original research and content to members' (www. abpco.org/about-abpco/). Having persuaded colleagues of its value, my role on the Executive Committee was to find the means of satisfying this aspiration.

My relationship with ABPCO started in the same way as it had done with the ITT. I interviewed a senior member of the Association for a project that led to Thomas and Thomas (2013). A short period of time later, I was in the process of creating an Advisory Board for the research centre that I had been appointed to lead (www.leedsbeckett.ac.uk/icreth/) and invited Jennifer Jenkins, then incoming Chair of ABPCO and Managing Director of MCI UK and Ireland, to join. She agreed and invited me to join ABPCO's Board with a view to making connections between academics and practitioners. Following her stepping down, Caroline Windsor and Nicole Leida became Co-Chairs and were equally enthusiastic about what became entitled the 'research connections' initiative. As an aside, it is interesting that working with universities to gain access to research topped the list in a membership survey conducted to inform the choice of priorities during one of the regular membership consultation exercises.

One of my initial roles at ABPCO was to deliver the keynote address at what was then termed the Annual Chairman's (sic) Lunch. I offered a somewhat pessimistic assessment of event management becoming a professionalised occupation (based on Thomas and Thomas 2013) unless new strategies were developed. This was well received and stimulated some interesting discussion among delegates. I was surprised to be complemented, without a hint of irony, by the Chair on bringing some rigour to the analysis of their strategy via the use of theory. The openness to new ideas was instructive but has not, in reality, altered the direction of the Association fundamentally. To that extent, the limited prospects of event management becoming a professionalised occupation remain.

The plan that emerged to strengthen collaboration between universities and industry via ABPCO involved several distinct activities. At the initial stage, there were no active academic members of ABPCO apart from me. The first involved creating a new membership category for university departments. The offer consisted of enabling easy access to research participants, creating an opportunity to bid for seedcorn research funding, effecting mechanisms to disseminate research and to promote continuous professional development (CPD) opportunities, assistance with sourcing guest speakers and use of the logo 'Courses recognised by ABPCO'. Within one year, this resulted in six universities joining. ABPCO, under my guidance, subsequently offered Centre of Excellence status to applicant departments that could meet a specified set of criteria. In 2016, the UK Centre for Events Management at Leeds Beckett University became the first ABPCO Centre of Excellence. This attracted significant coverage in the trade press (e.g. www.meetpie.com/Modules/NewsModule/NewsDetails.aspx?newsid=22300; www.gmiportal.com/index.php/63-gmi-news/2885-leeds-beckett-university-named-abpco-s-1st-centre-of-excellence).

The 'research connections' initiative involved encouraging academic researchers to propose projects that would align with the interests of ABPCO; to participate in 'engaged scholarship'. By doing so, they would secure modest grant funding but also gain access to participants and be assured of an audience beyond academia. A meeting attended by academics from nine universities took place in July 2015 (www.internationalmeetingsreview.com/united-kingdom/uk-universities-team-abpco-industry-research-101834). Three projects emerged as possibilities that were then reduced to two following further discussions. None of the associated researchers, however, applied for seedcorn funding. The identified projects remained no more than 'good ideas'.

Two round-table discussions, where academics presented their research to interested practitioners, took place in 2016 as part of an attempt to escalate engagement. I also agreed to speak at an association round-table event, reporting recent work on absorptive capacity in the meetings industry. The informal discussions that took place at these events were seen as encouraging by ABPCO but did not prompt additional research activity with (or without) impact. Again, academic engagement was welcomed but claims to impact would be tenuous at best.

One of the striking challenges of trying to maintain a flow of knowledge between universities and practitioners that goes beyond the education of students is not a lack of demand from a potentially interested audience but a shortage of (research) supply. Even where offers of financial and non-financial support are available, there is little take-up. This acts as a significant limiting factor to extensive research with impact related to this occupation(s) or sector of the economy.

CONCLUSION

Tourism professional associations have failed to professionalise occupations relating to travel, tourism, hospitality or events management in any sense that would be recognised as meaningful using contemporary conceptual frameworks. Their existence provides members with social and 'professional' benefits arising mainly from the networking opportunities that are made available. Academics can, but rarely do, gain access to these networks by joining the same associations. Even when they do join, however, this does not lead to research impact for the reasons discussed in this chapter and in Chapter 2; most managers appear not to be transformational learners and most learning takes place informally, largely on a peer-to-peer basis. The lack of high-quality academic research that is seen as credible, in that it recognises and draws upon the tacit knowledge of practitioners, compounds other barriers to impact. That academics continue to problematise issues in isolation from users and judge its value largely via publication in 'scientific' journals suggests that the situation will not change, even in the medium to long term. It is probable, instead, that instances of collaboration between academics and professional associations will continue to be celebrated but will represent no more than illusory narratives of impact.

References

Airey, D. (2016). Victor Middleton: Bridging theory and practice in tourism. *Anatolia, 27*(4), 577–583.

Burgess, C. (2011). Are hotel managers becoming more professional? The case of hotel financial controllers? *International Journal of Contemporary Hospitality Management, 23*(5), 681–695.

Dolnicar, S., Grabler, K., Grun, B., & Kulnig, A. (2011). The key drivers of airline loyalty. *Tourism Management, 32*(5), 1020–1026.

Formadi, K., & Raffai, C. (2009). New professionalism in the events sector and its impact in Hungary. In T. Baum, M. Deery, C. Hanlon, L. Lockstone, & K. Smith (Eds.), *People and work in events and conventions: A research perspective* (pp. 75–89). Walingford: CABI International.

Harris, V. (2004). Event management: A new profession? *Event Management, 9*, 103–109.

Haywood-Farmer, J., & Stuart, I. (1990). An instrument to measure the 'degree of professionalism' in a professional service. *The Service Industries Journal, 10*(2), 336–347.

Kipping, M. (2011). Hollow from the start? Image professionalism in management consulting. *Current Sociology, 59*(4), 530–550.

Lamoureux, K. M. (2017). Donald E. Hawkins: Transferring knowledge into practice. *Anatolia, 28*(4), 617–623.

McNamee, M. J., Sheridan, H., & Buswell, J. (2000). Paternalism, professionalism and public sector leisure provision: The boundaries of a leisure profession. *Leisure Studies, 19*, 199–209.

Mezirow, J. (2000). Learning to think like an adult: Core concepts of transformation theory. In J. Mezirow (Ed.), *Learning as transformation: Critical perspectives on a theory in progress* (pp. 3–33). San Francisco: Jossey-Bass.

Mezirow, J. (2009). Transformative learning theory. In J. Mezirow & W. Taylor (Eds.), *Transformative learning in practice: Insights from community, workplace and higher education* (pp. 18–32). San Francisco: Jossey-Bass.

Muzio, D., & Kirkpatrick, I. (2011). Introduction: Professions and organisations: A conceptual framework. *Current Sociology, 59*(4), 389–405.

Muzio, D., Hodgson, D., Faulconbridge, J., Beaverstock, J., & Hall, S. (2011). Towards corporate professionalization: The case of project management, management consultancy and executive search. *Current Sociology, 59*(4), 443–464.

Rhoden, S., Ralston, R., & Ineson, E. M. (2008). Cabin crew training to control disruptive airline passenger behaviour: A cause for tourism concern? *Tourism Management, 29*(3), 538–547.

Schafer, A., Heywood, J. B., Jacoby, H. D., & Waitz, I. A. (2009). *Transportation in a climate-constrained world*. Cambridge, MA: MIT Press.

Sheldon, P. J. (1989). Professionalism in tourism and hospitality. *Annals of Tourism Research, 16*(4), 492–503.

Thomas, H. (1991). Professionalism, power and planners. In H. Thomas & P. Healey (Eds.), *Dilemmas of planning practice* (pp. 34–47). Aldershot: Avebury.

Thomas, R. (2007). *Professionalism in travel and tourism* (Institute of Travel and Tourism Research Report 1). Hertfordshire: ITT.

Thomas, R. (2008). *Attitudes to climate change: A survey of travel agents and tour operators* (Institute of Travel and Tourism Research Report 2). Hertfordshire: ITT.

Thomas, R. (2009). *Flexible working practices in travel and tourism* (Institute of Travel and Tourism Research Report 3). Hertfordshire: ITT.

Thomas, R. (2012). Business elites, universities and knowledge transfer in tourism. *Tourism Management, 33*(3), 553–561.

Thomas, R. (2013). Research and scholarship with impact: A British perspective. *Worldwide Hospitality and Tourism Themes, 5*(3), 277–282.

Thomas, R., & Thomas, H. (2013). What are the prospects for professionalizing events management in the UK? *Tourism Management Perspectives, 6*, 8–14.

Thomas, R., & Thomas, H. (2014). 'Hollow from the start?' Professional associations and the professionalization of tourism in the UK. *The Service Industries Journal, 34*(1), 38–55.

Van de Ven, A. (2007). *Engaged scholarship a guide for organizational and social research*. Oxford: Oxford University Press.

Wen, I. (2009). Factors affecting the online travel buying decision: A review. *International Journal of Contemporary Hospitality Management, 21*(6), 752–765.

CHAPTER 4

The Impact of Academics on Policy and Practice

If every tourism academic died tomorrow,
the tourism industry would not notice.
Research professor interviewed for this book

Abstract Following the Introduction, this chapter reviews Thomas and Ormerod's (Tourism Manage 62:379–389, 2017a) study which traced the digital footprint of all academics returned as part of a tourism submission to the Research Excellence Framework (REF) in 2014. It compares commonly used indicators of academic quality (notably citations) with potential indicators of impact (such as citations by non-academics to academic work) to inform a discussion on the relative difference in non-academic impact between academics. REF impact templates and case studies, and interview data with research-active academics and REF panel members, complement the analysis. The chapter concludes by arguing that the limited non-academic impact of tourism scholarship is not explained by forms of market failure but by recognising that universities, tourism businesses and tourism policy-makers operate within marginal and largely separate (but well defined) communities of practice.

Keywords Tourism studies · Universities · Impact

R. Thomas, *Questioning the Assessment of Research Impact*, Palgrave Critical University Studies, https://doi.org/10.1007/978-3-319-95723-4_4

67

INTRODUCTION

It is not surprising that impressive, and perhaps exaggerated, claims are made nowadays by many researchers about their influence on non-academic practice. To contend otherwise might jeopardise their ability to secure research funding, hamper their promotion prospects and even attract the opprobrium of those managing submissions to performance-based research funding evaluation exercises such as the Research Excellence Framework (REF). As has been discussed in Chapter 1, such evaluations now feature increasingly as part of research funding regimes in many parts of the (neoliberal) world, e.g. Australia (www.arc.gov.au/excellence-research-australia), Canada (Albert and McGuire 2014), New Zealand (www.tec.govt.nz/funding/funding-and-performance/funding/fund-finder/performance-based-research-fund/) and the UK (see www.ref.ac.uk/). Banal-Estanol et al. (2015: 1160) encapsulated this when they commented recently that 'nowadays, increasing university–industry collaboration is a primary policy aim in most developed economies'. (For further discussion of issues related to the growing emphasis on 'relevance', see Bramwell et al. 2016; Coles 2009; Geuna and Piolatto 2016; Glover 2015; Hill and Kumar 2009; Tartari et al. 2012.)

Research policy in the UK does not distinguish, in principle, between disciplines or fields of study when setting expectations for research impact. Moreover, differences between sectors of the economy or policy domains do not influence this aspect of research policy. What are often described as knowledge-intensive (technical) industries underpins conceptualisations of university–industry relations. Yet, similar expectations are placed on academics whose work is of potential relevance only to those operating in what are regularly seen as low value-added, sluggish and marginal sectors of the economy. It is interesting that official descriptions of these sectors change when there are perceived political gains to be made from, for example, hosting major sports or cultural events or when significant amounts of public spending on such events is to be justified (Foley et al. 2012; Smith 2012). As has been argued in Chapters 2 and 3, it is likely that the dynamics of knowledge flows and utilisation vary significantly between industries. An important consequence of this is that academics working on projects with commercial possibilities are, for example, faced with the same requirement to justify the public value of their work as those who are not (perhaps ever able to).

This chapter examines empirically the impact of UK-based tourism academics on policy and practice. Drawing heavily on the work of Thomas and Ormerod (2017a), it first traces the digital footprint of all academics returned as part of a tourism submission to the REF in 2014 (see also Wood 2017; Thomas and Ormerod 2017b). They did this using publicly available information (such as the REF submissions and those unearthed via searches of the internet) to identify the digital footprint of the UK's leading tourism researchers. By comparing commonly used indicators of academic quality (notably citations) with potential indicators of impact (such as citations by policy-makers to academic work), they develop profiles of academics with greatest impact. The analysis then identifies reasons for differential levels of non-academic impact. The chapter also considers two additional sources of empirical material. The first comes from the impact templates and case studies submitted to REF 2014 in the UK. The second is comprised of seventeen interviews undertaken with researchers and REF panel members.

A COMMENT ON MEDIATORS AND MECHANISMS FOR KNOWLEDGE EXCHANGE

The literature is replete with proposals for creating productive collaborative arrangements between universities and other organisations to advance knowledge exchange (for a recent review, see de Wit-de Vries et al. 2018). Indeed, a significant amount of effort continues to be expended seeking answers to questions about the relative value of contractual arrangements between these actors compared with looser forms of cooperation (e.g. Vega-Jurado et al. 2017; Etzkowitz and Zhou 2018). Typically, studies focus upon STEM (science, technology, engineering, mathematics) (Bozeman et al. 2013, 2015). Collaboration is never assured and, at times, relationships lead to inter-university and university–industry conflict, often related to matters of financial gain (e.g. Sherkow 2016).

Boyer's (1997) influential work on academic scholarship provides the starting point for conceptualising some of the more prominent mechanisms and mediators of impact. It is evident that certain categories of scholarship are more likely to yield commercial collaboration; for example, 'discovery research' would probably be more interesting to those seeking a financial return via the mediating role of venture capital investors or a roll-out company, but other categories may also lead to non-academic impact. Figure 4.1 represents a range of possibilities and is modified from that provided by Bastow et al. (2014). As they suggest, advances in the social sciences are usually both incremental and collaborative. Thus, it is difficult to identify transformational developments identifiable to one source. In terms of impact, therefore, strong regimes of appropriability (see Chapter 2) are unlikely to obtain and any 'first mover advantages' are likely to be limited.

Even among STEM academics, the evidence of research impact is mixed. Referring to their research on the work of academic engineering scientists, some commentators recently noted that the:

> collaboration-publication relationship could be described by an inverted U-shaped curve .... Links with the private sector may boost research output because collaboration can provide new ideas and additional funding. But high degrees of collaboration can also damage research output. (Banal-Estanol et al. 2015: 1173)

Banal-Estanol et al. (2015) also draw attention to related studies which produced contradictory evidence. From this, they identify several potentially important individual and organisational variables that are likely to influence impact (see also Perkmann et al. 2013).

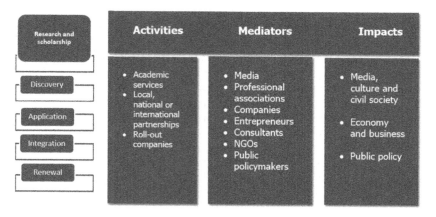

Fig. 4.1 Potential flow and impact of tourism research (*Source* Thomas and Ormerod [2017a] as adapted from Bastow et al. [2014: 25])

There has, to date, been little modelling of the non-academic impact of social scientists' research. One of the few comprehensive studies found that, what they called, 'core' social scientists were more likely to generate impact (or at least to have their work noticed by non-academic audiences) if they were older (up to a point), worked in certain locations (probably enabling greater access to key 'stakeholders'), were a professor and had a Ph.D., and were visible on the web. Perhaps most striking, however, is the 'distinct link between scholars generating excellent academic research and publications and having concentrated external impacts ... so (they argue) ... the processes involved in researching, engagement with external organisations or sectors, and publishing, all enhance both aspects' (Bastow et al. 2014: 103). Unfortunately, Bastow et al. (2014) say very little about individual disciplines or fields of study apart from signalling that significant differences exist and that each is worthy of separate empirical analysis.

There is a growing interest in notions of open innovation and co-creation in tourism (see, e.g., Shaw 2015). Hoarau and Kline (2014) are, however, among the few commentators to explore the innovation process in tourism that encompasses co-creation between university academics and practitioners. They paint a picture of product, managerial, institutional and process innovations emerging from collaborative work among Icelandic and Norwegian whale watching tour operators and marine scientists. The engagement they describe is presented as exemplifying how tacit and explicit knowledge may be shared by both parties. The apparently fertile conditions that exist in these cases allowed mutual benefits to emerge for the scientists and the commercial tour operators. For all its insight, however, the paper does not speculate about how tourism academics and their research, rather than marine biologists, might resonate with practitioners in a similar fashion.

What is seen by Pyo (2005, 2011) as the dissonance between the knowledge requirements of destination managers and the knowledge produced by academics might be resolved by the so-called needs gap-kano-prioritisation procedure. This approach informs the research agenda of academics by prioritising the knowledge needs of practitioners. The stated advantages are illustrated via South Korean case studies, suggesting the importance of spatial considerations in practitioner research agenda setting. Corroborating evidence for the potential value of this form of collaboration appears in the form of Pyo's (2011) subsequent work and that of Ankrah et al. (2013), though the latter might be seen as more predictable as it attracted public funding (representing a subsidy to the collaboration). One of the major benefits claimed of Pyo's work is that research funding at destinations can be used more effectively and efficiently. However, as Thomas and Ormerod (2017a: 382) argue:

> In many developed economies, resources available for research within destinations is often sparse. The universal application of Pyo's model is, therefore, difficult to imagine for a substantial number of destinations. As the funding of academic research often takes place within a national framework and the responsibility for ensuring that research projects make an impact on practice lies with individual academics and university departments, the strategies of engagement adopted are, generally, far more personalised and institutionally specific than appears to be the case in South Korea.

Moreover, as has been argued in Chapter 2, explanations for the innovativeness (and competitiveness) of commercial or non-commercial organisations in tourism do not usually include a key role for universities.

A Note on What Is Written About (and How)

As non-academic impact has become an important dimension of funded research in the UK, it is reasonable to suppose that increasingly sophisticated policy or practice recommendations would be reflected in academic writing. Indeed, this might be especially so for journals whose missions lay claim to improving tourism policy or practice. Although the sample is small and the choice of volume arbitrary, the material contained in Table 4.1 is instructive by way of a backdrop to the subsequent discussion.

The two journals listed in Table 4.1 claim to be concerned, in part, with effecting change: *The Journal of Sustainable Tourism* is a leading international journal which welcomes 'new ideas and approaches in relation to the theory and practice linking tourism and sustainability' (http://www. tandfonline.com/action/journalInformation?show=aimsScope&journalCode=rsus20); notwithstanding its emphasis on critical public policy studies, *The Journal of Policy Research in Tourism, Leisure and Events*, draws attention to the fact that its work has been cited in Organisation for Economic Cooperation and Development (OECD) documents as a means of promoting its 'relevance' (http://www.tandfonline.com/action/journalInformation?show=aimsScope&journalCode=rprt20).

Table 4.1 Policy or practice orientation of articles in two tourism journals with impact potential (2017)

Author(s)	Title	Indication of practice or policy contribution
Journal of Sustainable Tourism		
Fairer-Wessels (2017)	Determining the impact of information on rural livelihoods and sustainable tourism development near protected areas in Kwa-Zulu Natal, South Africa	The study concludes that, where it is a matter of survival for rural communities, a sustainable livelihoods approach may be more appropriate and attainable than a sustainable tourism development approach (p. 10)
Font and Hindley (2017)	Understanding tourists' reactance to the threat of a loss of freedom to travel due to climate change: a new alternative approach to encouraging nuanced behavioural change	If nothing else, this study is further proof of the complexity of engaging consumers in the protection of the environment and may partly explain the failures of some pro-environmental behaviour campaigns. It shows how, collectively, we require a better understanding of consumer behaviour in relation to motivations, which is far more complex (p. 38)
Gunter et al. (2017)	Ecotourism and economic development in Central America and the Caribbean	This approach would further allow the issue of convergence to steady-state growth paths to be investigated (p. 57)
Zhang et al. (2017)	Creating a scale for assessing socially sustainable tourism	The theoretical and managerial implications of the scale are discussed, including options for annual surveys giving policymakers alerts before situations worsen (p. 61)
Hayes et al. (2017)	Impacts of recreational diving on hawksbill sea turtle (*Eretmochelys imbricata*) behaviour in a marine protected area	MPA managers should collaborate with key stakeholders and researchers to implement monitoring programmes that assess the impacts of tourism on natural resources. The current study has been an initial effort toward meeting this objective (p. 92)
Becken et al. (2017)	Urban air pollution in China: destination image and risk perceptions	… this paper concludes that unless China proactively addresses the problem of air pollution, for example by seeking to stimulate positive feelings, international arrivals may continue to be compromised (p. 130)

(continued)

Table 4.1 (continued)

Author(s)	Title	Indication of practice or policy contribution
Clavé and Wilson (2017)	The evolution of coastal tourism destinations: a path plasticity perspective on tourism urbanisation	*The article argues for a wider range of social and cultural criteria in the analysis of tourism evolution_advocating the use of path plasticity and a cultural political economy approach_to offer an alternative perspective on shifting tourism situations, reflecting the inherently "urbanising" nature of tourism development in the traditional coastal resort context* (p. 96)
Boley et al. (2017)	Gender and empowerment: assessing discrepancies using the resident empowerment through tourism scale	*For practitioners, the application of the RETS provides a concrete example of how to directly test for empowerment discrepancies between men and women as well as on other socio-demographic factors, such as age, race, income and education.... allows tourism industry managers and other government officials the opportunity to identify problem areas and subsequently modify tourism marketing and management plans ...* (pp. 124–125)
Collins and Cooper (2017)	Measuring and managing the environmental impact of festivals: the contribution of the Ecological Footprint	*The paper demonstrates that Ecological Footprint analysis can provide valuable information for festival organisers and policy-makers on factors influencing the scale of a festivals' environmental impact, and the types of strategies needed to reduce the effect of visitor travel* (p. 148)
Journal of Policy Research in Tourism, Leisure and Events		
Elshaer and Saad (2017)	Political instability and tourism in Egypt: exploring survivors' attitudes after downsizing	*It is also important, for managers, to understand possible changes in survivors' everyday work interactions and their effect on the organizational goals. This may guide managers to the need to change or develop current HR practices or programs to suit survivors' new attitudes and behaviors at work* (p. 18)

(continued)

Table 4.1 (continued)

Author(s)	Title	Indication of practice or policy contribution
Farajat et al. (2017)	Addressing travel writers' role as risk brokers: the case of Jordan	… a practical level, it is essential for the JTB to provide the invited travel writers with timely public safety information and encourage them to share this information in their travel articles (p. 36)
Basnyat et al. (2017)	Political instability and trade union practices in Nepalese hotels	The study contributes to our understanding of the fragility of industrial relations within the tourism industry in Nepal, and how this can be exacerbated in an environment characterized by ongoing instability (p. 40)
Afonso-Rodríguez (2017)	Evaluating the dynamics and impact of terrorist attacks on tourism and economic growth for Turkey	Despite the possible drawbacks of the proxy used, we obtain significant and consistent evidence on the negative impact of terrorist activity on economic growth for Turkey through the deterioration of the long-run relationship between tourism and economic growth (pp. 76–77)
Deep and Johnston (2017)	Travel advisories—destabilising diplomacy in disguise	In the paper, we advance five models we believe help generalise our discussion to a wider range of cases. The paper thus has significant practical implications for countries being adversely affected by politically and economically motivated travel advisories (p. 82)
Ivanov et al. (2017)	Impacts of political instability on the tourism industry in Ukraine	… that illustrates the impact of the political instability on the tourism industry, as well as elaborates the tactics that hoteliers and travel agency managers in Ukraine are taking to counteract the shock (p. 100)

Readers will reach their own judgement about the likely value of these papers to those concerned with practical policy-making and other decision-making within commercial and non-commercial contexts. None of the papers provide much obvious evidence of being written by 'engaged scholars' (Van de Ven 2007) or of being driven by those seeking a resolution to a practical set of problems. As is discussed at various points elsewhere in the book, the notion of being 'engaged' in this sense carries with it an ontological, methodological and epistemological perspective that elevates the value of collaboration with actors as a means of gaining 'better' insight. This might then usefully inform contemporary policy or organisational challenges. The observations made about Table 4.1 are not surprising nor intended to be a judgement of the papers' academic value. Each of the journals uses a rigorous process of peer review and is concerned to maintain or to achieve a reputation for academic rigour. However, the closing comments highlighted from the papers listed in the table suggest that espoused editorial aspirations result in few contributions with more than seemingly perfunctory considerations of 'implications'. It is possible, of course, that 'translation exercises' take place and that impact is far greater than these papers imply. The evidence considered below suggests otherwise.

THE ACADEMICS' DIGITAL FOOTPRINT

The incidence of tourism academics' work appearing on the websites of non-academic organisations provided Thomas and Ormerod (2017a) with the data required for what they call the 'collective digital footprint' for academic tourism research in the UK. Figure 4.2 compared their data with those provided by Bastow et al. (2014) for social science and STEM researchers. It is noteworthy that the data on tourism researchers encompasses only the relatively elite group that were deemed worthy enough by their institutional colleagues to be nominated for assessment (REF 2014).

Figure 4.2 shows the incidence of website references to academic work organised into three categories devised by Bastow et al. (2014): 'traditional academic', the 'mediating middle' and 'external society'. The first of these refers to university and other academic websites. The data presented reveal a smaller proportion of total website references for tourism researchers, leading to the suggestion that the work of academics in this marginal field might be cited more prominently by non-academics compared with social science more generally and STEM subjects.

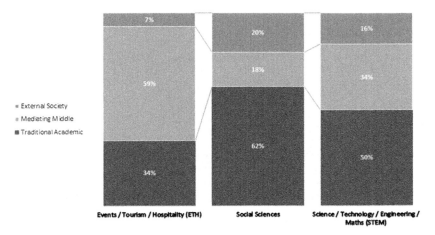

Fig. 4.2 The digital footprint of tourism, social science and STEM academics (*Source* Adapted from Thomas and Ormerod [2017a])

The broadly defined 'mediating middle' includes intermediaries who communicate academic research or draw attention to its existence. The media would fall within this category as would professional associations. The significantly larger proportion of tourism work in this category implies a collective output that resonates with audiences beyond universities.

The third category, 'external society', is the one most directly relevant to the arguments developed in this book because it conveys the proportion of digital citations by non-academic constituencies. Contrary to the emerging picture described above, the particularly low proportion of work in this category for tourism scholars indicates a body of work that has a considerably smaller impact on non-academics than social science and STEM.

Thomas and Ormerod (2017a) explain how difficult it was to find references to academic work on non-tourism websites (see Table 4.2). Indeed, they needed to review 300 search results to be sure of capturing the appropriate data (typically, studies of this kind limit their searches to 100). As they say, 'The most striking feature of the searches was, therefore, the very low incidence of academic work being referred to by others' (Thomas and Ormerod 2017a: 385).

The next section shifts attention from the collective footprint to the impact of individual academics on non-academic constituencies.

Table 4.2   References to academic research or researchers by non-academic actors and agencies

Number of references	Number of academics	%
0	8	7
1–5	32	29
6–25	65	59
26–50	6	5
N	111	100

Source Open Google searches reported in Thomas and Ormerod (2017a: 385)

MODELLING ACADEMIC IMPACT IN MARGINAL FIELDS

The central challenge driving Thomas and Ormerod's (2017a) contribution was the desire to identify the reasons for some academic researchers enjoying greater non-academic impact than others. The starting point of their analysis established the academic impact of all researchers returned in REF 2014 and the factors that determined such impact. Those with an interest in the detail of their approach are referred to their original work. For the purposes of this book, suffice to say that Table 4.3 contains the results of their Negative Binominal Regression (NBR) analyses using three measures of academic impact (the average number of citations during the REF auditing period, their highest cited article during the same period and total citations) and the explanatory (independent) variables which were supposed to be responsible for the differential levels of impact.

To help interpret the data, it should be noted that the incidence rate ratio (IIR) indicates the probability of a unit increase in a positive direction if the number is above 1 in the independent variable precipitated by a change in the dependent variable. SE is the standard error for each IIR, i.e. the extent to which the result might have arisen by chance. The strongest relationships are highlighted in bold.

Table 4.3 confirms what many would expect. A professorial post, the possession of a Ph.D. and being older all strengthen academic impact. Working with co-authors also appears to increase citations (perhaps as a result of simply having more outputs or because the authors attract different constituencies).

Although the data show many interesting insights, the connection between academic and non-academic impact (total citations and references to their work on non-academic websites) is initially the most important.

Thomas and Ormerod (2017a) went on to examine the characteristics of academic researchers with the greatest non-academic impact as evidenced by citations to them or their work on non-academic websites. The variables used were those utilised to explain academic impact but they now became the independent variables (justified from their reading of the literature).

Table 4.3 Regression analysis of factors associated with academic impact

Independent variables	Dependent variable: academic impact					
	Average citations (all outputs) (2008–2015)		Top cited article		Total citations (excluding self-citations)	
	Regression 1		Regression 2		Regression 3	
	IRR	SE	IRR	SE	IRR	SE
Academic position (Professor = 1)	1.69***	(0.19)	2.79***	(0.21)	1.92***	(0.20)
Region (London = 1)	0.85	(0.31)	1.09	(0.36)	1.28	(0.40)
Highest qualification (Ph.D. = 1)	0.92	(0.31)	1.55	(0.38)	3.02**	(0.45)
Years since academic's highest qualification	1.01	(0.14)	0.99	(0.02)	1.02	(0.18)
Status of academic current institution (RG = 1)	0.747	(0.31)	1.01	(0.36)	1.69	(0.36)
Average number of co-authors (outputs 2008–2015)	1.25**	(0.99)	1.29**	(0.13)	0.77*	(0.14)
Total external mentions outside of academia	0.99*	(0.01)	0.99	(0.01)	1.04***	(0.12)
Status of highest qualification institution (RG = 1)	0.88	(0.19)	0.96	(0.22)	1.06	(0.24)
LinkedIn (Yes = 1)	0.97	(0.17)	0.90	(0.20)	0.82	(0.21)
Twitter (Yes = 1)	0.95	(0.22)	1.71*	(0.30)	1.67*	(0.27)
Webpage/blog (Yes = 1)	0.86	(0.31)	0.83	(0.38)	0.69	(0.33)
University web profile (Yes = 1)	0.75	(0.42)	0.68	(0.50)	0.68	(0.53)
Online CV (Yes = 1)	1.46	(0.36)	1.18	(0.43)	2.09*	(0.41)
Membership of external associations/organisations (Yes = 1)	1.35	(0.19)	1.40	(0.22)	1.03	(0.23)

(continued)

Table 4.3   (continued)

Independent variables	Dependent variable: academic impact					
	Average citations (all outputs) (2008–2015)		Top cited article		Total citations (excluding self-citations)	
	Regression 1		Regression 2		Regression 3	
	IRR	SE	IRR	SE	IRR	SE
Positions of external responsibility (Yes = 1)	1.17	(0.19)	1.14	(0.22)	1.09	(0.22)
Age 2015	1.03	(0.25)	1.10***	(0.32)	1.03	(0.04)
Age²	1.00*	(0.00)	1.00**	(0.00)	1.00	(0.00)
Gender (Male = 1)	1.12	(0.16)	1.08	(0.19)	1.16	(0.20)
Nationality (British = 1)	1.32*	(0.16)	0.83	(0.20)	1.63**	(0.20)
Model significance	0.00		0.00		0.00	
Log likelihood	−409.47		−609.64		−372.41	
Dispersion indicator	0.38		0.59		0.57	

Significant at ***$p \le .01$, **$p \le .05$, and *$p \le .10$
IRR = Incidence rate ratio
SE = Standard error
Source Thomas and Ormerod (2017a: 385)

Table 4.4 shows the findings of three regressions used to build an explanation of the impact of academic researchers on non-academic actors. The same dependent variable was used but additional independent variables were added to strengthen the modelling. As the table shows, the two most statistically significant variables influencing non-academic impact are (a) the article most cited by fellow academics during the REF audit period and (b) total outputs (see Regressions 5 and 6). Even in these cases, however, the effects are moderate (e.g. the probability of an additional paper increasing external profile was only 3% though there may be a cumulative effect which would enhance the external visibility of prolific authors). Similarly, low levels of probability are attached to age as a statistically significant predictor of impact on non-academic constituencies. Collectively, the results suggest that researchers who are well established and prolific appeal most to practitioner and other non-academic audiences.

Table 4.4 Regression analysis of factors associated with external impact

Independent variables	Dependent variable: external impact					
	Regression 4		Regression 5		Regression 6	
	IRR	SE	IRR	SE	IRR	SE
Total publications (2008–2015)			1.03***	(0.01)	1.03***	(0.01)
Total citations (excluding self-citation) (not limited to review period)			1.00	(0.01)	1.01	(0.01)
Average citations (all publications 2008–2015)			1.00	(0.01)	1.00	(0.01)
Top cited article (2008–2015)			1.00**	(0.01)	1.00**	(0.00)
Academic position (Professor = 1)	1.34	(0.22)	1.04	(0.23)	1.03	(0.22)
Region (London = 1)	1.30	(0.37)	1.19	(0.33)	1.18	(0.33)
Highest qualification (Ph.D. = 1)	2.51**	(0.43)	1.78	(0.40)	1.77	(0.40)
Years since academic's highest qualification	1.00	(0.02)	0.99	(0.02)	0.99	(0.02)
Status of academic current institution (RG = 1)			1.18	(0.33)	1.17	(0.34)
Average number of co-authors (outputs 2008–2015)					1.03	(0.12)
Status of highest qualification institution (RG = 1)			1.06	(0.21)	1.06	(0.20)
LinkedIn (Yes = 1)			0.97	(0.18)	0.98	(0.18)
Twitter (Yes = 1)			1.36	(0.22)	1.37	(0.22)
Webpage/blog (Yes = 1)			1.49	(0.26)	1.49	(0.26)
University web profile (Yes = 1)			0.81	(0.47)	0.79	(0.47)
Online CV (Yes = 1)			0.90	(0.32)	0.89	(0.32)
Membership of external associations/organisations (Yes = 1)	1.25	(0.19)	1.30	(0.18)	1.28	(0.19)
Positions of external responsibility (Yes = 1)	1.43*	(0.19)	1.29	(0.18)	1.30	(0.19)

(continued)

Table 4.4   (continued)

Independent variables	Dependent variable: external impact					
	Regression 4		Regression 5		Regression 6	
	IRR	SE	IRR	SE	IRR	SE
Age 2015	1.02	(0.35)	1.09**	(0.04)	1.09**	(0.04)
Age^2	1.00	(0.00)	1.00**	(0.00)	1.00**	(0.00)
Gender (Male = 1)	0.96	(0.18)	0.79	(0.17)	0.79	(0.17)
Nationality (British = 1)	0.84	(0.18)	0.74*	(0.16)	0.74*	(0.17)
Model significance	0.04		0.00		0.00	
Log likelihood	−361.38		−344.58		−344.54	
Dispersion indicator	0.56		0.38		0.38	

Significant at ***$p \leq .01$;,**$p \leq .05$, and *$p \leq .10$
IRR = Incidence rate ratio
SE = Standard error
Source Thomas and Ormerod (2017a: 386)

The following paragraph summarises the key findings of Thomas and Ormerod's (2017a: 387) study in relation to non-academic impact:

> There are several sets of activities undertaken by academics that are designed to promote impact. The two most prominent among tourism scholars relate to their utilisation of social media and practitioner networks. Contrary to some received wisdom, the evidence from this study suggests that while the former may generate 'attention', to a large extent this is 'noticed' mainly by fellow academics. It is helpful, therefore, in enhancing academic rather than non-academic profiles. While there is evidence of impact arising from engagement with practitioner networks, this activity is also a poor predictor of impact when attention shifts from isolated examples... individual characteristics also play a role in achieving academic and non-academic impact, notably in relation to age. This is to be expected as 'age' probably reflects a gaining of experience, expertise, an ability to act more autonomously and an accumulated body of work. All of these strengthen an academic's profile and probably enable them to engage more effectively with their peers and external agents, when opportunities arise.

The picture to emerge thus far is one where the impact of academic tourism research is generally low and that the key drivers to impact appear not to be activities such as sustained use of social media for promotional purposes (cf. Badgett 2015; Carrigan 2016; Reed 2016) but a consistent undertaking of high-quality work as judged by academic peers.

What Do the REF Case Studies Teach Us?

British universities submitted 9 case studies to explain the impact of their research on tourism to Unit 26 (Sport and Exercise Sciences, Leisure and Tourism) and 6 to Unit 19 (Business and Management Studies). For many, this will seem a relatively small number for an established field that, for this exercise, encompassed event management and hospitality management. Elsewhere in Unit 26, for example, there were a total of 128 claims to impact made, most of which focused on aspects of sport and sports science. In Unit 19, there were 432 in total.

The number of case studies each institution was eligible to submit depended upon the number of staff nominated for assessment. At the time of submission, it was clear to those involved in taking selectivity decisions that the volume and composition of the group to be assessed depended upon a combination of the availability of good quality research outputs (to achieve a good grade point average or GPA) and the implications this had for the number of case studies expected by the funding council. The University of Surrey, for example, submitted 14.4 members of staff to Unit 26 from a School complement of potentially 26 or more academic staff (excluding those on teaching only contracts). Leeds Beckett University submitted 48.6 from a much larger staff base but a minority of these were tourism scholars. As a result of the number of staff returned, these institutions submitted 2 and 6 case studies, respectively. There is substantial anecdotal evidence that some submissions were smaller than they might have been because research managers were concerned that they did not have enough impact case studies to match outputs. This potential dilemma applied to all Units of Assessment.

Table 4.5 summarises the submitted case studies relating to tourism. Most are available for inspection at http://results.ref.ac.uk/. Between them, they deal with a range of issues but there is a cluster of work on tourism economics, the environment and sustainability more generally, and a set of social (welfare) concerns. Much of the research on which the case studies draw is inter- or multidisciplinary but there is also a significant disciplinary contribution, mainly from economics. Most institutions claim to inform public policy but some state that the private sector and NGOs have used the research referred to as a means of informing their policies and practices. Varied evidence is provided to support the claims made. For the purposes of this analysis, they have been grouped into four categories.

Table 4.5 REF 2014 impact case studies

Institution	Unit	Title	Approach[a]	Major claim	Evidence		
					Cited in official report(s)	Cited in media	Invitation to join network (temporary or over longer term)	Other (e.g. letter of support or artefact)
Cardiff University	19	Understanding the economic and environmental impacts of tourism	Investment in impact and planned engagement	'...significantly contributed to developing methodologies to quantify tourism's socio-economic impact at different scales Their development of the first Tourism Satellite Account for the UK has informed the way national and international agencies conceptualise and measure tourism impacts...'	✓	✓	✓	✓
University of Exeter	19	Social marketing and sustainability: influencing policy and practice for consumer engagement	Strategic partnerships with stakeholders, investing in growth areas and facilitating impact through support mechanisms	'...three types of impact, relating to changes in government policy, product development for SMEs and informed public debate'	✓	✓	–	–

(continued)

Table 4.5 (continued)

Institution	Unit	Title	Approach[a]	Major claim	Evidence			
					Cited in official report(s)	Cited in media	Invitation to join network (temporary or over longer term)	Other (e.g. letter of support or artefact)
University of Kent	19	Backpackers or cruise ships? Shaping the tourism policy agenda for small island states and coastal communities	Applied research centres and internal support mechanisms (including research and impact manager)	'…inform tourism policy for the world's 40 small island developing states (SIDS) and poor coastal communities'	✓	–	✓	–
University of Nottingham	19	Informing social tourism policy and practice	Raising awareness, developing skills and allocating resources, establishing advisory boards and other long term partnerships, creative approaches to dissemination	'The research informed policy debate in an all-party parliamentary report and subsequently Visit England's domestic tourism strategy. The work led to changes in the charity's practices, leading to new systems, services and strategy'	✓	✓	✓	✓

(continued)

Table 4.5 (continued)

Institution	Unit	Title	Approach[a]	Major claim	Evidence			
					Cited in official report(s)	Cited in media	Invitation to join network (temporary or over longer term)	Other (e.g. letter of support or artefact)
Oxford Brookes University	19	Academic–industry collaboration in risk management: a case study in the hospitality sector	Conduct research that relates to wider concerns, institutional resources allocated to achieve impact	'…(research) has strengthened practices in a turbulent business environment. … pioneered a partnership … resulting in the Group developing new risk management practices, enhancing its effectiveness in managing risks, saving costs and gaining worldwide recognition as industry leader in the field…'	–	✓	–	✓
York St. John University	19	Corporate social responsibility. The disclosure–performance gap	Participate in research events and engage with professional bodies and businesses in UK and internationally	'the results of the study were presented at the Internationale Tourismus Borse (ITB) in Berlin 2011 (a major global trade fair)…according to the lead author…'plenty of anecdotal evidence' of the impact the study has had on the industry'	–	✓	–	–

(continued)

Table 4.5 (continued)

Institution	Unit	Title	Approach[a]	Major claim	Evidence Cited in official report(s)	Cited in media	Invitation to join network (temporary or over or longer term)	Other (e.g. letter of support or artefact)
University of Bedfordshire	26	The impact of food tourism on sustainable development in rural regions	Prioritise research relating to sustainable development and climate change, and economic impact and regeneration	'...the results have been used ... to inform ...Food Tourism Strategy for the Causeway Coast and Glens region of North Ulster in Northern Ireland and the Brecon Beacons National park Food Strategy in Wales ...The Irish Tourist Board ...has also used the research ...'	✓	–	–	✓
Bournemouth University	26	Modelling economic impact for national governments	Engaging with industry e.g. via match funded Ph.D. bursaries, supporting staff (including funding impact activities), shaping policy discourses, public engagement e.g. via blogs, talks, or twitter	'The models and modelling approaches ... have fed into the development of tourism-related and general economic policies by a number of international organisations, national governments and public authorities of various ranks'	✓	✓	✓	✓

(continued)

Table 4.5 (continued)

Institution	Unit	Title	Approach[a]	Major claim	Evidence			
					Cited in official report(s)	Cited in media	Invitation to join network (temporary or over longer term)	Other (e.g. letter of support or artefact)
Bournemouth University	26	Details unavailable						
University of Brighton	26	Redesigning tourism policy and practices in Africa	Undertake applied multidisciplinary research, emphasise collaboration, interventions, support for staff and infrastructure to enable impact	'Researchers at the University of Brighton have changed national tourism policy and workforce training practices in African countries'	✓	✓	–	✓
University of Kent	26	Informing public debate and policy-makers on the Olympic Games legacy	Support for staff (training and resources) to achieve impact	'By challenging conventional wisdom on the health legacy of sporting mega-events … stimulated and informed public debate in the UK and abroad… research has also had demonstrable impact on key policymakers…'	✓	–	✓	✓

(continued)

Table 4.5 (continued)

Institution	Unit	Title	Approach[a]	Major claim	Evidence			
					Cited in official report(s)	Cited in media	Invitation to join network (temporary or over longer term)	Other (e.g. letter of support or arte-fact)
Sheffield Hallam University	26	The economic and social impacts of major events and festivals	Engage regularly with non-academics and develop 'rich partnerships'	'The main impacts … derive from the setting up of the eventsimpacts website in 2010…it is common practice for evaluation contracts to specify that the outputs must be eventsimpacts.com compliant'	–	–	–	✓
University of Sunderland	26	Integrated e-services for advanced access to heritage in cultural tourist destinations (ISAAC)	Collaboration, embedding impacts in research, dissemination beyond academic audiences	'…enhance the relationship between heritage and tourism in urban destinations through a novel Information Communication Technology (ICT) environment'	✓	–	–	✓

(continued)

Table 4.5 (continued)

Institution	Unit	Title	Approach[a]	Major claim	Evidence			
					Cited in official report(s)	Cited in media	Invitation to join network (temporary or over longer term)	Other (e.g. letter of support or artefact)
University of Surrey	26	Reducing social exclusion through participation in tourism	Long-term partnerships with international agencies and networks, collaboration via studentships, practitioner training	'Our research has led to changes in behaviour and action of either demand or supply with the main beneficiaries being people with disabilities, low-income groups, tourism businesses and policy makers'	✓	–		✓
University of Surrey	26	Modelling and forecasting international tourism demand: methodological advancements and innovations	Long-term partnerships with international agencies and networks, collaboration via studentships, practitioner training	'The main beneficiaries of our research are the organisations that commissioned the team to conduct consultancy projects or directly adopted our forecasting methodologies and reports'	✓	–	✓	

[a]Typically, this relates to a wider research group such as a business school or a department that includes sports scientists

Source http://results.ref.ac.uk/

The first evidential form is to point out that the research has been cited in official reports. It may, or may not, be more than an acknowledgement but it confirms that influential audiences at least know of the existence of the research. The second is being quoted in the media. Again, the respectability of press coverage has a certain cache but does not necessarily (though it might) equate with impact. Indeed, it may even be a poor proxy because those familiar with the operations of the media will know that accuracy of reports about academic research is generally poor. Moreover, the media are not always as discriminating about who they ask to comment and do not usually check the credentials of those offering 'expert' comment (which contributes to an impression at times that some of the insights reportedly made by academics stretch credibility). The third source of evidence is broadly associated with invitations to join networks. This affords academic members the opportunity to influence others (see Chapter 3 for a discussion of why this is not inevitable). The final category of evidence encompasses testimonials, letters of support or artefacts such as smartphone apps.

Individual case study scores are not published. However, it is clear that at least some of the research reported in the case studies produced what is now deemed officially to be 'outstanding impacts in terms of their reach and significance'. This deduction is possible because some submissions only contained tourism case studies. This applied to submissions from Bournemouth University, the University of Surrey and the University of Sunderland. Their respective profiles for impact were 60% four star and 40% three star; 40% four star, 40% three star and 20% two star; and 100% two star, respectively. It is not possible to know the scores of other institutions because in all other cases, the tourism case studies were contained within wider submissions.

The criteria and process of official assessment are transparent but the conversations between panel members are confidential. Although there is feedback, this tends to be relatively general. It is not possible to know precisely, therefore, why certain scores were given. It is interesting, however, that the two submissions with the highest impact listed on Table 4.6 included technical work on economic modelling and utilised several sources of evidence. The former is consistent with one of the central arguments of this book, i.e. because the sector is not knowledge intensive and most research undertaken by tourism academics is not seen as overly technical, it has little impact.

Table 4.6 Average impact profile for Units 19 and 26

	4 star	3 star	2 star	1star	Unclassified
Unit 19	37.7	42.5	17	2.2	0.6
Unit 26	39.2	32.4	21.8	6.3	0.3

Source http://results.ref.ac.uk/Results/ByUoa/26

Table 4.6 reports the average impact profiles for Units 19 and 26. This suggests that about three quarters of the impact case studies generated a significant impact, i.e. made a positive contribution by changing aspects of the work of practitioners and policy-makers. To accept this uncritically is naïve. There are several reasons why the impact profile was generally high: (i) it was the first research assessment exercise to consider impact and, as a result, expectations may have been lower than for, say, quality of outputs; (ii) assessment was undertaken by a panel dominated by academics who were selected for their ability to make judgements about the quality of research outputs; (iii) other panel members were recruited from outside academia and were expected to judge the influence of academic work. Interview data suggest that panel members were learning how to make such assessments because of the lack of precedents. More importantly, the evidence base on which judgements were made rested on what was provided by institutions themselves. It is evident that this 'tracking forward' approach produces more favourable impressions than when 'tracking back' (i.e. starting with the user). Studies undertaken for the ESRC using the latter did not always replicate the pictures painted by academics (e.g. Parsons and Thomas 2015a, b; Parsons et al. 2014). This was usually because practitioners reported a much more complex set of information flows and influences, drawing on multiple sources, than those provided by universities.

Arguably, one mark of an academic researcher's impact is his or her ability to attract income from those it seeks to influence. If a commercial enterprise or a public body is prepared to pay for the expertise of researchers, they may value—and by inference use—the findings more willingly. The argument is extended, anecdotally, to peer-reviewed funding; if the unit is successful in attracting peer-reviewed funding, such as that from research councils, it may be a marker of quality, which may in turn influence impact. Table 4.7 summarises the funding sources reported in the impact case studies.

The evidence presented in the case studies indicates that researchers in tourism attract relatively little funding overall. There are some notable

Table 4.7 REF 2014 case studies: External sources of funding

Institution	Unit	Title of case study	Amount		Source					
			>£20,000 c29,000 USD	<£20,000 c29,000 USD	**Research council (or similar) peer reviewed research grant**	Research council other	European Union	Commercial	Other	No funding details given or details unclear
Cardiff University	19	Understanding the economic and environmental impacts of tourism	–	–	–	–	–	–	–	✓
University of Exeter	19	Social marketing and sustainability: influencing policy and practice for consumer engagement	2	3	2	1	0	0	2	
University of Kent	19	Backpackers or cruise ships? Shaping the tourism policy agenda for small island states and coastal communities	–	2	2	–	–	–	–	

(continued)

Table 4.7 (continued)

Institution	Unit	Title of case study	Amount		Source					
			>£20,000 c29,000 USD	<£20,000 c29,000 USD	Research council (or similar) peer reviewed research grant	Research council other	European Union	Commercial	Other	No funding details given or details unclear
University of Nottingham	19	Informing social tourism policy and practice	2	–	1	1	–	–	1	
Oxford Brookes University	19	Academic-industry collaboration in risk management: a case study in the hospitality sector	–	–	–	–	–	–	–	✓
York St. John University	19	Corporate social responsibility. The disclosure–performance gap	–	–	–	–	–	–	–	✓
University of Bedfordshire	26	The impact of food tourism on sustainable development in rural regions	–	–	–	–	–	–	–	✓

(continued)

Table 4.7 (continued)

| Institution | Unit | Title of case study | Amount | | Source | | | | | |
			>£20,000 c29,000 USD	<£20,000 c29,000 USD	Research council (or similar) peer reviewed research grant	Research council other	European Union	Commercial	Other	No funding details given or details unclear
Bournemouth University	26	Modelling economic impact for national governments	4	4	–	–	–	2	6	–
Bournemouth University	26	Details unavailable	–	–	–	–	–	–	–	–
University of Brighton	26	Redesigning tourism policy and practices in Africa	1	–	1	–	–	–	–	–
University of Kent	26	Informing public debate and policy-makers on the Olympic Games legacy	–	–	–	–	–	–	–	✓
Sheffield Hallam University	26	The economic and social impacts of major events and festivals	5	–	–	–	–	–	5	–

(continued)

Table 4.7 (continued)

Institution	Unit	Title of case study	Amount		Source					
			>£20,000 c29,000 USD	<£20,000 c29,000 USD	Research council (or similar) peer reviewed research grant	Research council other	European Union	Commercial	Other	No funding details given or details unclear
University of Sunderland	26	Integrated e-Services for Advanced Access to Heritage in Cultural Tourist Destinations (ISAAC)	1	–	–	–	1	–	–	–
University of Surrey	26	Reducing social exclusion through participation in tourism								
University of Surrey	26	Modelling and forecasting international tourism demand: methodological advancements and innovations								

Source http://results.ref.ac.uk/

exceptions, where key individuals attract significant amounts of research council funding but these are rare. Commercial funding is also modest in its incidence. That probably suggests that practitioners and policy-makers do not see academic institutions as the places to which they would naturally turn to help address their problems. Several of those interviewed corroborated this perspective. The discussion of research quality is considered further in Chapter 5.

CONCLUSION

This chapter has argued that the non-academic impact of UK-based university researchers working in the academically marginal fields of tourism and related subjects is almost imperceptible. It began by suggesting that the imperative to publish research that is judged by their peers to be theoretically sophisticated and empirically robust leads tourism academics to deliver research outputs that are of limited practical relevance. This was illustrated briefly by reviewing papers published in the first issue of 2017 of two journals that claim to have a positive disposition towards work of relevance to policy-makers or other practitioners. This was followed by an analysis of publicly available data from REF 2014 and a review of Thomas and Ormerod's (2017a) comprehensive empirical assessment of the non-academic impact of tourism scholars.

The chapter also discussed models of research user engagement that exist in other fields, notably those relating to STEM subjects. These begin to show why the crude application of a universal model of impact is unlikely to yield the results aspired to by policymakers. The discussion also reveals parts of a wider argument advanced in this book, namely that the non-academic impact of tourism scholars is unlikely to change in the near future. There are several reasons for this: (i) the quality of research in tourism and related fields is improving but progress is slow; (ii) because tourism research takes place almost exclusively in non-research-intensive universities, levels of investment in research are lower than in their research-intensive counterparts; (iii) the need to engage a sector that does not consider the insights of academic research to be important to their ability to innovate or become more competitive (as was explained in Chapters 2 and 3) makes achieving impact especially elusive. Perhaps of greatest disappointment to protagonists of tourism research impact is the very limited likelihood of improvements to funding which might hasten development. Indeed, there are reasonable expectations that current higher education (and research) funding will diminish or be distributed in a manner that favours other disciplines or fields of study (IFS 2017; Williams 2017; https://www.timeshighereducation.com/news/pm-may-announces-major-review-english-university-funding).

REFERENCES

Afonso-Rodríguez, J. A. (2017). Evaluating the dynamics and impact of terrorist attacks on tourism and economic growth for Turkey. *Journal of Policy Research in Tourism, Leisure and Events, 9*(1), 56–81.

Albert, M., & McGuire, W. (2014). Understanding change in academic knowledge production in a neoliberal era. In S. Frickel & D. J. Hess (Eds.), *Political power and social theory: Volume 27. Fields of knowledge: Science, politics and publics in the neoliberal age* (pp. 33–57). Bingley: Emerald Group Publishing Limited.

Ankrah, S. N., Burgess, T. F., Grimashaw, P., & Shaw, N. E. (2013). Asking both university and industry actors about their engagement in knowledge transfer: What single-group studies of motives omit. *Technovation, 33*, 50–65.

Badgett, M. V. L. (2015). *The public professor: How to use your research to change the world.* New York: New York University Press.

Banal-Estanol, A., Bonet-Jofre, M., & Lawson, C. (2015). The double-edged sword of industry collaboration: Evidence from engineering academics in the UK. *Research Policy, 44,* 1100–1175.

Basnyat, S., Lovelock, B., & Carr, N. (2017). Political instability and trade union practices in Nepalese hotels. *Journal of Policy Research in Tourism, Leisure and Events, 9*(1), 40–55.

Bastow, S., Dunleavy, P., & Tinkler, J. (2014). *The impact of the social sciences.* London: Sage.

Becken, S., Jin, X., Zhang, C., & Gao, J. (2017). Urban air pollution in China: Destination image and risk perceptions. *Journal of Sustainable Tourism, 25*(1), 130–147.

Boley, B. B., Ayscue, E., Maruyama, N., & Woosnam, K. M. (2017). Gender and empowerment: Assessing discrepancies using the resident empowerment through tourism scale. *Journal of Sustainable Tourism, 25*(1), 113–129.

Boyer, E. L. (1997). *Scholarship reconsidered: Priorities for the professoriate.* London: Wiley.

Bozeman, B., Fay, D., & Slade, C. P. (2013). Research collaboration in universities and academic entrepreneurship: The state-of-the art. *Journal of Technology Transfer, 38,* 1–67.

Bozeman, B., Gaughan, M., Youtie, J., Slade, C. P., & Rimes, H. (2015). Research collaboration experiences, good and bad: Dispatches from the front lines. *Science and Public Policy.* https://doi.org/10.1093/scipol/scv035.

Bramwell, B., Higham, J., Lane, B., & Miller, G. (2016). Advocacy or neutrality? Disseminating research findings and driving toward sustainable tourism in a fast changing world. *Journal of Sustainable Tourism, 24*(1), 1–7.

Carrigan, M. (2016). *Social media for academics.* London: Sage.

Clavé, S. A., & Julie Wilson, J. (2017). The evolution of coastal tourism destinations: A path plasticity perspective on tourism urbanisation. *Journal of Sustainable Tourism, 25*(1), 96–112.

Coles, T. (2009). Tourism studies and the governance of higher education in the United Kingdom. *Tourism Geographies, 11*(1), 23–42.

Collins, A., & Cooper, C. (2017). Measuring and managing the environmental impact of festivals: The contribution of the Ecological Footprint. *Journal of Sustainable Tourism, 25*(1), 148–162.

Deep, A., & Johnston, C. S. (2017). Travel advisories—Destabilising diplomacy in disguise. *Journal of Policy Research in Tourism, Leisure and Events, 9*(1), 82–99.

de Wit-de Vries, E., Dolfsma, W. A., van der Windt, H. J., & Gerkema, M. P. (2018). Knowledge transfer in university-industry research partnerships: A review. *Journal of Technology Transfer.* https://doi.org/10.1007/s10961-018-9660-x.

Elshaer, I. A., & Saad, S. K. (2017). Political instability and tourism in Egypt: Exploring survivors' attitudes after downsizing. *Journal of Policy Research in Tourism, Leisure and Events, 9*(1), 3–22.

Etzkowitz, H., & Zhou, C. (2018). *The triple helix: University-industry innovation and entrepreneurship* (2nd ed.). Abingdon: Routledge.

Fairer-Wessels, F. A. (2017). Determining the impact of information on rural livelihoods and sustainable tourism development near protected areas in Kwa-Zulu Natal, South Africa. *Journal of Sustainable Tourism, 25*(1), 10–25.

Farajat, S. A. D., Liu, B., & Pennington-Gray, L. (2017). Addressing travel writers' role as risk brokers: The case of Jordan. *Journal of Policy Research in Tourism, Leisure and Events, 9*(1), 23–39.

Foley, M., McGillivray, D., & McPherson, G. (2012). *Event policy.* London: Routeldge.

Font, X., & Hindley, A. (2017). Understanding tourists' reactance to the threat of a loss of freedom to travel due to climate change: A new alternative approach to encouraging nuanced behavioural change. *Journal of Sustainable Tourism, 25*(1), 26–42.

Geuna, A., & Piolatto, M. (2016). Research assessment in the UK and Italy: Costly and difficult, but probably worth it (at least for a while). *Research Policy, 45,* 260–271.

Glover, T. D. (2015). Leisure research for social impact. *Journal of Leisure Research, 47*(1), 1–14.

Gunter, U., Ceddia, M. G., & Tröster, B. (2017). International ecotourism and economic development in Central America and the Caribbean. *Journal of Sustainable Tourism, 25*(1), 43–60.

Hayes, C. T., Baumbach, D. S., Juma, D., & Dunbar, S. G. (2017). Impacts of recreational diving on hawksbill sea turtle (*Eretmochelys imbricata*) behaviour in a marine protected area. *Journal of Sustainable Tourism, 25*(1), 79–95.

Hill, D., & Kumar, R. (Eds.). (2009). *Global neoliberalism and education and its consequences.* London: Routledge.

Hoarau, H., & Kline, C. (2014). Science and industry: Sharing knowledge. *Annals of Tourism Research, 46*, 44–61.

Institute for Fiscal Studies (IFS). (2017). Higher education funding in England: Past, present and options for the future. IFS Briefing Note BN211. London: IFS/ESRC.

Ivanov, S., Gavrilina, M., Webster, C., & Ralko, V. (2017). Impacts of political instability on the tourism industry in Ukraine. *Journal of Policy Research in Tourism, Leisure and Events, 9*(1), 100–127.

Parsons, D., & Thomas, R. (2015a). *Evaluating the economic impact of social science: Pilot study of impact 'valuation'.* Swindon: Economic and Social Research Council (ESRC).

Parsons, D., & Thomas, R. (2015b). *Evaluating the economic impact of social science: Summary report for the ESRC.* Swindon: Economic and Social Research Council (ESRC).

Parsons, D., Thomas, R. Strange, I., & Walsh, K. (2014). *Evaluating the impact of economics centres.* Swindon: Economic and Social Research Council (ESRC).

Perkmann, M., Tartari, V., McKelvey, M., Autio, E., Brostrom, A., D'Este, P., et al. (2013). Academic engagement and commercialisation: A review of the literature on university-industry relations. *Research Policy, 42*, 243–442.

Pyo, S. (2005). Knowledge map for tourist destinations—Needs and implications. *Tourism Management, 26*(4), 583–594.

Pyo, S. (2011). Identifying and prioritizing destination knowledge needs. *Annals of Tourism Research, 39*(2), 1156–1175.

Reed, M. S. (2016). *The research impact handbook.* Huntley: Fast Track Impact.

Research Excellence Framework (REF). (2014). *Research Excellence Framework 2014: The results.* London: HEFCE; Edinburgh: SFC; Cardiff: HEFCW; and London: Department for Employment and Learning.

Research Excellence Framework (REF). (2015). *Research Excellence Framework 2014: Overview report by Main Panel C and Sub-panels 16–26.* London: HEFCE; Edinburgh: SFC; Cardiff: HEFCW; and London: Department for Employment and Learning.

Shaw, G. (2015). Tourism networks, knowledge dynamics and co-creation. In M. McLeod & R. Vaughan (Eds.), *Knowledge networks and tourism* (pp. 45–61). London: Routledge.

Sherkow, J. S. (2016). Pursuit of profit poisons collaboration: The CRISPR-Cas9 patent battle demonstrates how overzealous efforts to commercialize technology can damage science. *Nature, 532*(7598), 172–173.

Smith, A. (2012). *Events and urban regeneration.* London: Routledge.

Tartari, V., Salter, A., & D'Este, P. (2012). Crossing the Rubicon: Exploring the factors that shape academics' perceptions of the barriers to working with industry. *Cambridge Journal of Economics,* 655–677.

Thomas, R., & Ormerod, N. (2017a). The (almost) imperceptible impact of tourism research on policy and practice. *Tourism Management, 62,* 379–389.

Thomas, R., & Ormerod, N. (2017b). Founts of knowledge or delusions of grandeur? Limits and illusions of tourism research impact: A reply to Wood. *Tourism Management, 62,* 394–395.

Van de Ven, A. H. (2007). *Engaged scholarship: A guide for organizational and social research.* Oxford: Oxford University Press.

Verga-Jurado, J., Kask, S., & Manjarres-Henriquez, L. (2017). University industry links and product innovation: Cooperate or contract? *Journal of Technology Management and Innovation, 12*(3), 1–8.

Williams, G. (2017). The United Kingdom divided: Contested income-contingent student loans. In D. Palfreyman, T. Tapper, & S. Thomas (Eds.), *Towards the private funding of higher education: Ideological and political struggles.* Abingdon: Routledge.

Wood, R. C. (2017). The unspoken question: A response to Thomas and Ormerod. *Tourism Management, 62,* 390–393.

Zhang, H. Q., Fan, X. F. D., Tse, S. M. T., & King, B. (2017). Creating a scale for assessing socially sustainable tourism. *Journal of Sustainable Tourism, 25*(1), 61–78.

CHAPTER 5

Reacting to the Impact Agenda: Performativity and a 'New Collegiality'

Not everyone tries. That is up to them… Because people don't, that is why not many of us have the respect of industry.
Senior researcher interviewed for this book

I've seen the inexorable rise in impact and I can see what it's doing to working cultures, demands on staff, producing new kinds of internal hierarchies etc. And yet I am advising PhDs and post docs about developing impact because I know the job market is so tough they need to be on top of this.
Research professor interviewed for this book

Abstract This chapter considers the response to the impact agenda of academic researchers working in the marginal fields of tourism and related subjects. Drawing on interview data garnered from a selection of well-established researchers, including REF panel members, it finds extensive evidence of individualistic career-related performativity and widespread participation in what others have called a 'new collegiality' (a system of control that emphasises competition with academics external to their workplace). Notwithstanding research orientations that often emphasise the economically liberating role of tourism, or its contribution to intercultural understanding and social improvement, there was little evidence of progressive or critical performativity. An important casualty of the growing focus on impact among those interviewed appears to be

© The Author(s) 2018
R. Thomas, *Questioning the Assessment of Research Impact*, Palgrave Critical University Studies,
https://doi.org/10.1007/978-3-319-95723-4_5

the reduced emphasis given to the teaching of students. This is argued to be damaging because it undermines a potentially more fruitful alternative activity, namely research to inform teaching.

Keywords Tourism studies · Universities · Work

INTRODUCTION

This chapter considers how British academics working in marginal subjects, in this case tourism and related fields, are responding to the impact agenda. As with similar performance-based funding regimes, researchers are increasingly required to develop narratives to explain how their research effects positive change in the practices of non-academic constituencies or in public debate. Using the language of research councils, this involves planning 'pathways to impact' (http://www.rcuk.ac.uk/innovation/impacts/). Whether academic researchers consider the inclusion of impact a welcome or damaging development is discussed as is the effect this aspect of research policy is having on their approach to academic work.

Four observations are worthy of note before proceeding. Firstly, it has been established in Chapter 4 that the non-academic impact of academic research in tourism is low. Even where social media are used ardently for promotional purposes, they influence academic impact rather than being noticed by practitioners and policy-makers (Thomas and Ormerod 2017). As one senior research professor noted somewhat magniloquently during interview: 'If every tourism academic died tomorrow, the tourism industry would not notice'.

Secondly, the idea of a golden age of higher education is often used as a benchmark when commenting (negatively) on current research policy and the working lives of university academics. As Thomas (2005: 242) reminds us, however:

> modern academic life has probably always been an awkward mix of competition and collegiality, combined with a dose of venality… novels such as Kingsley Amis's *Lucky Jim* … or sociological analyses of higher education … should persuade us that there was no golden age where the pursuit of truth took precedence over personal ambitions, and dispassionate scholarly endeavour was the sole object of academic life, universally acclaimed and always justly rewarded.

Thirdly, universities have long been associated with questions of economic competitiveness, innovation and vocational education (Ruegg 2004). As discussed in Chapter 1, successive governments of industrialised countries have for generations emphasised the role of, and spoken of investment in, universities to develop new technologies and to produce a highly skilled workforce. In this broad sense, the link between university research and economic performance is not new.

Finally, the idea that universities have long emphasised published research outputs, as opposed to scholarship, at the expense of teaching does not stand up to close historical scrutiny (Slee 1986; Smyth 2017). As has been discussed at various points elsewhere in the book, however, contemporary approaches to the management of neoliberal universities, coupled with technological advances, have led to greater emphasis on 'performance' and the use of transparent metrics. This has had a distinctive effect on the working lives of academic researchers by influencing where, about what and how often they publish their work. It has also altered perceptions of teaching and the amount of time dedicated to preparing for and engaging in that activity. For researchers in British universities, a similar process of cultural transformation with respect to impact is palpable.

The contrasting missions and histories of universities have implications for how academic researchers approach their work. Regardless of their missions, however, it is evident that many institutions are facing similar pressures and appear to be drawing on a relatively narrow menu of managerial options (Watts 2017). In the UK, most tourism research takes place in 'modern' (post 1992) universities. Only one research-intensive university (Surrey), itself a relative newcomer (established in 1966), has a critical mass of tourism students and researchers. It is noteworthy that even in this case, only 14.4 full-time equivalent staff were submitted for evaluation in the last REF (http://results.ref.ac.uk/Results/BySubmission/1475).

The analysis that follows draws upon formal interviews with seventeen academic researchers undertaken for the purposes of this book. It is also a product of many hours of informal conversations with fellow academics at seminars and conferences; the latter included international events where I was able to test evolving perspectives (e.g. Thomas 2017a, b). Commissioned evaluations of impact and exploratory studies to help conceptualise and measure impact undertaken with Professor David Parsons and, more latterly, Dr. Neil Ormerod, for the Economic and

Social Research Council (ESRC) will also have influenced my thinking. That said, the meanings ascribed to the views expressed during interviews and conversations are mine alone.

PERSPECTIVES ON IMPACT

There is widespread acceptance among the tourism academics interviewed for this book that there are benefits to be gained from engaging with non-academic audiences. Even those with concerns over how to generate impact do not often question the legitimacy of the requirement. This may be a reflection of the nature of tourism research and its antecedents (Airey et al. 2015), or of the structural characteristics of the sector (Thomas et al. 2011). More likely, however, is that it merely mirrors a similar conformity to that found elsewhere in British universities across a range of disciplines (Watts 2017). The following comments illustrate the perception of many:

> If you had asked me 10 years ago, I would have said no, but increasingly I do think it matters. I do think we need to have more impact.

And

> Well, the first thing to say is that I am much more conscious these days of audiences than I ever was before. You know, I think in the early days you write things because you have got that intrinsic interest, you've got a driving need to say something about a subject, or to discover the answer to a question... These days, it's much more at the top of my mind about, well, who's going to listen to this, or who's going to be interested in it? ... And part of that is the REF (Research Excellence Framework) ... To be honest with you, I'm an advocate of it... I'm not really into doing research just for its own sake, or just because it's of interest to me. I have done that in the past but I'm much more interested in thinking about 'How might this be used? Is it going to be of any use to anybody? And in what way might it be useful?'

There is very little questioning of the appropriateness of a research policy which increasingly emphasises impact. Even those offering a critical perspective seem to accept the principle:

> I know some people still say 'Oh, impact, a load of rubbish.' I don't think that at all. I think it has always been really important to think about what you do with the results of your work. How do you get the results of your

research to the people who will be interested in it? So in one way you can say think about impact as a way of thinking through those questions. What are you going to do with your research? Who is going to read it? What difference is it going to make? All really good questions to think about, in principle. And then at some point you have got to try and then do a separate exercise, which is make sure those questions are answered in a way that meets the impact requirements. But I see that as a kind of pragmatic adjustment to something that you should be thinking about anyway.

Each of these passages is interesting because they align the behaviour of the academic precisely with changes in research policy. The distinction drawn between research driven by intrinsic interest and for non-academic impact is common, conspicuously relegating, largely by omission, any (important) connection between teaching and research.

Quite predictably, the extent to which academic researchers feel they have achieved impact varies:

> ... it's difficult to then measure, or even see, impact. And I agree, in most of my work in tourism... I can't say, hand on heart, 'Yeah, that's had impact.' I can't.

By contrast:

> I would say (I have been) relatively successful (at achieving impact) but I have not been very good at collecting data or evidence of that.... Because a number of people have expressed - unsolicitedly expressed - their opinion that they have changed their mind about something...

Several of those interviewed intimated the kind of constraints to impact identified more systematically by others in the literature (Bartunek and Rynes 2014; Melissen and Koens 2016; Thomas 2012). Thus, interviewees tended not to problematise the issue as part of a wider critique of a neoliberal system of higher education but concentrated on explaining one or two practical issues they felt prevented them from achieving impact. To that extent, most of those interviewed considered the pursuit of impact to be benign, almost only a technical challenge, which might be overcome with greater effort and investment in a set of more effective communicative practices.

Although not stated explicitly by many of those interviewed, the acquisition of a particular set of skills does not appear to represent a major impediment to achieving impact. The barriers to impact are, apparently, often to be found in the deficiencies of others (including actors who do not 'recognise' the usefulness of academic work or are unable to appreciate and react to its complexity and insight). As the following illustrates, many adopted Melissen and Koens' (2016: 2) arguably somewhat presumptuous tone, when they lament the fact that 'insights developed in academia have not always resulted in *progress* in practice' (emphasis added):

> *Academic:* It (industry) needs to sort of think more about how it uses academic research and academic outputs a bit more pro-actively and engage with academic tourism studies.
>
> *Interviewer:* Does it?
>
> *Academic:* Well, I don't know whether it does or not, but I think it needs to.
>
> *Interviewer:* Why does it need to?
>
> *Academic:* Well, because it needs to improve their skills; it needs to create a bit more of a refined conversation with policymakers, rather than just sort of blunt instruments, you know 'let's hit the policymakers with, if they don't do this now, if they don't change the visa laws now it's going to have a big cash impact.' There needs to be a better connecting set of arguments that takes a bit more of a helicopter view. I don't think the industry is in a position to do that, unless it has better, more well-informed and more rounded people working in it.

Such a perspective almost imagines rational business decision-making and policy-making processes, free from prejudice, whereby the valuable knowledge produced by academics might be brought to bear to reach effective decisions. The evidence presented in Chapters 2 and 3 suggests otherwise. Indeed, the conspicuous failure of British academics to influence tourism policy, or even, to help co-construct a research agenda with policy-makers surely shatters such illusions. Theoretical explanations of public policy-making, and available empirical evidence, assume greater ambiguity, complexity, a privileging of those with power and a degree of policy-failure. All of these challenge academic researchers seeking to influence non-academic actors and test the plausibility of their ambitions.

The effect on academic workloads of adding impact to what Kyvik (2013) calls the growing list of tasks associated with the role of being an academic researcher was noted by some. This work intensification was seen as a constraint to impact; the perception of being 'stretched' (Clarke and Knights 2015) was a much more problematic issue than any reorientation of academic work:

> So, I think that largely it's brought a lot of stress to people who've got enough pressure to deal with already. On the other hand, I think that it is right to push people to think about what the point is of the work that they are doing. I think it is too easy to just put your head down and piddle away with your own little pet project without thinking about what it means for the big wide world. So I think in that sense it **can** have value, and it can be really (be) effective, when you think about, you know, 'I've done this research, there's no point just putting it in a drawer, how do I actually make sure it actually lives a life?' I think that is really positive.

Again, this confirms that even the critics interviewed expressed a degree of approbation for research policy that emphasises (the, largely, collectively unachieved) non-academic impact. This is not necessarily the case for other fields (Watermeyer 2016).

PERFORMATIVITY BUT LITTLE THAT WAS ANTI-, PROGRESSIVE OR CRITICAL

Academic researchers do not present a uniform response to the research impact agenda. Nevertheless, the similarities in the portraits they paint of academic work, with a common concern for performativity, are striking. Some, perhaps many, share the employment insecurities identified by Knights and Clarke (2014) and an interest in career advancement (Clarke and Knights 2015). Identification of these characteristics is not new or confined to those operating at the academic margins of higher education in the UK. Commentators interested in the academic identities and practices of those working in the British education system have, for some time, highlighted the centrality of 'performativity' (Macfarlane 2016; Smyth 2017; Page 2017). As Gond et al. (2016) discuss in their systematic review of the literature, the term is used differently by social scientists and this is explained by contrasting foundational conceptualisations. These need not be examined here; performativity is used in this chapter in terms explained by Ball (2012: 19):

> (it is) a powerful and insidious policy technology that is now at work at all levels and in all kinds of education and public service, a technology that links effort, values, purposes and self-understanding to measures and

comparisons of output ....In regimes of performativity experience is nothing, productivity is everything. Last year's efforts are a benchmark for improvement – more publications, more research grants, more students. We must keep up; strive to achieve the new and very more diverse targets which we set for ourselves in appraisal meetings; confess and confront our weaknesses; undertake appropriate and value-enhancing professional development; and take up opportunities for making ourselves more productive .... We take responsibility for working hard, faster and better as part of our sense of personal worth and the worth of others.

The following verbatim comments portray the contrasting ways in which performativity inflected the discussions with those interviewed:

> I probably have not been strategic about things like that, and I have only wanted to produce things that I thought... where I had something to say. So I have not played the game, you know .... Yes. I suppose I just have not ever really played this game properly, particularly on citations and all those issues.

As another stated:

> Well, I think there are games that you have to play... so I just have to be pragmatic, I think, and just accept that if people think that journal rankings mean something and impact factors means something, and publishing something that's a bit more theoretical means something as well...(it) legitimises me in the academic community – justifies that I belong here. And then there is doing something that has practical value, that gives me more personal satisfaction... Maybe because we are in the kind of field that we are not exactly clear what research in tourism is all about and what our purpose really is, then we still have this debate, 'Well, is this applied work or is this theoretical work?' ... I have made a choice of being able... wanting to play both sides. And almost constantly feeling that whatever you publish isn't very good, because it did one thing but not the other. And you're thinking, it's going to be a bit difficult to try to get it to do both. I think they have different audiences.

Clearly, there were critical voices when discussing impact but none of those interviewed reflected what some commentators have described as 'anti-performativity', i.e. the rejection of producing knowledge designed to maximise efficiency in various, usually economic, spheres coupled with a strategy of non-compliance (Fournier and Grey 2000). Instead, fatalistic dispositions towards impact pervade the responses of those interviewed and take precedence over any apprehensions:

> No. I think the objection is to the kind of auditing process, which is so crudely defined. It is a bit like REF in itself, isn't it? It is designed with a certain kind of research in mind, you know, nature, basically, and everyone else will fit with that model. Which does not work for us at all, it is pointless. But there we are, we're stuck with it. You have to be pragmatic on one side, but still be true to your research aims on the other. *So it is a matter of working out a way in which you can get them to coincide and not compete.* (emphasis added)

and

> I kind of despair of the very restrictive view of impact that seems to be at work ... for them impact is all about can you show there is a direct economic benefit. And if you can, well, where's the kind of ... 'costed' benefit in terms of improving a policy. So I think for some very narrow fields (like mine) (for those) who are good at playing that game, it is a good game to be in. I think for me, as someone who's kind of a social scientist who thinks of trying to change the world, trying to make it more ethical and less driven by profit, I think I am on a hiding to nothing ... *I do try (to achieve impact).* (emphasis added)

It is also somewhat surprising, perhaps, that few researchers provided even a loose sense of progressive (Wickert and Schaefer 2015) or critical performativity (Spicer et al. 2009, 2016). The literature associated with these perspectives emphasises the potential role of academics as subversive voices seeking to 'raise the critical consciousness of actors in order to provide spaces in which new practices can be "talked into existence" through the performative effects of language' (Wickert and Schaefer 2015: 107). Despite research orientations that frequently emphasise the economically liberating role of tourism, or its contribution to intercultural understanding and social improvement, interviewees rarely produced coherent strategies for challenging norms. Indeed, even among those who claimed to be working 'on' or with 'movers and shakers' in corporate social responsibility departments, there was little sophisticated thinking that extended beyond their self-declared worldliness about how they might achieve the 'improvement' they desire. Perhaps most surprising, however, was the lack of reference to the debates on anti- or critical performativity among the 'critical social scientists' (those who often position their work under the broad heading of critical tourism/leisure/hospitality studies). This suggests a lack of familiarity with the radical thinking on impact (or creating the illusion of impact) taking place in other fields and disciplines (e.g. Gond et al. 2016; Wickert and Schaefer 2015; Spicer et al. 2016).

Similar observations might be made of the limited range of philosophical perspectives expressed in relation to knowledge construction when considered in the context of debates on impact. None of those interviewed appeared to have given any consideration to ontologies and epistemologies that would sit comfortably with achieving impact, even those most vociferous in their support of research policy. Commentators such as Van de Ven (2007), for example, have long argued that impact is constrained by the processes of knowledge production that predominate in universities, proposing a participative approach to scholarship leading to more rigorous (and relevant) insights into complex social problems. The point here is not to advocate such a position but to highlight the lack of consideration given to well-documented approaches to social and organisational research where impact is not a subsequent activity but is a central concern.

CAREERISM AND A 'NEW' COLLEGIALITY

Following the discussion of performativity, it is perhaps predictable that the interviews with researchers revealed widespread evidence of the careerism identified by Clarke and Knights (2015). They argue that in return for compliance with the demands of neoliberal research policy, academics accept the proposition that there are significant benefits available for achieving 'excellence' (which now encompasses achieving impact). They go on to show that participation in this apparently transparent, value-free, metric-led, meritocratic reward system leads some to what Ryan (2012) calls 'hyperindividualism' (see also Chapter 1). Notwithstanding the inherent limitations of interview data, this resonates with the comments made by some participants. Naturally, the number of individuals who can achieve the heady heights of achievement in each metric is, by definition, limited and potentially leads to individual senses of self-aggrandisement or failure, in this case in relation to impact:

.. And my worry is that a lot of the people that are against the whole idea of doing purposeful research ... They want to keep working in their ivory tower and nobody ever asking them for being accountable for their time... because otherwise you wrote it for, basically, psychological masturbation... just for your personal pleasure.

and

Not everyone tries. That is up to them. Impact does not just happen. You have to work at it, spend time with people and sell them the idea that we have something to show them. Because people don't, that is why not many of us have the respect of industry.

The interviews also highlighted support for collaboration between academics within the same institution. By so doing, it enabled departments to promote coherent programmes of research and a shop window of integrated specialists. Some have suggested that the performance-based funding system operating in the UK combines pressures for individualism with the need to present shared stories of interdisciplinarity as appropriate credentials for 'pitching' to undertake socio-economically beneficial research. In a discussion of city and regional planning academics, Thomas (2005: 243), for example, refers to this 'new collegiality' as being characterised by academic tribalism, where the pursuit of knowledge is subservient to the need for a narrative that justifies additional funding.

This is exemplified by the following comment made in relation to impact:

So I basically work the room. I go round talking to people, trying to see what we can do with each one of them. So I suppose I am a little bit calculated with that. But I just think we are not going to (succeed).. otherwise, and I see it as part of my job to achieve some of that. So I know I play the game. And some of the things, I just think I really wish somebody else would do that. So all the work I do on LinkedIn and Facebook and Twitter and YouTube and ResearchGate and academia.com... I don't know, it is just a way of trying to raise our profile, of what we are trying to do here collectively

And

This is now a team game. It has to be about our coherence and not the ramblings of mavericks, however good they are or think they are. We need to make a difference and to shout about it.

Those resistant to this 'collegiality' are often 'othered':

> And I think the problem is we have earned ourselves a reputation and we have worked really hard to earn the reputation that what we do is too slow, too little, too irrelevant, too conceptual, and does not really provide something to industry that they can work with. Our timeframes are completely different. The way in which we work is different. They will ask us for a piece of work and our answer is 'Let me go and do a literature review about that and then in four months' time I'll get an ethics form written up. And maybe in a year's time I can give you some preliminary results.' No. No, I do not think so....

> The bigger problem is that those academics have not identified industry, government, society, as their audience. They have not written the work in a way that they thought that affecting change is something that was part of their mandate. They have never thought who should read it and what they should do as a result of reading it.

Another stated:

> But also it made me realise that lots of the academics who I knew and who I kind of admire, they didn't realise what the relevant things were in the industry.

The fear of 'not letting the side down' was one of the factors identified by Thomas (2011) as preventing him from writing a critical paper on tourism policy-making, having (unusually) gained access as a participant to the process. His unease at colleagues' potential reactions contributed to a self-censorship. In related vein, Thomas (2010) shows how local coalitions gain advantage from the 'independent' narrative that universities are able to offer. The concerns are not that universities invent or manipulate data but that researchers are dissuaded subtly from asking too many (awkward) questions about the prevailing discourses for fear of withdrawal of funding or cooperative relationships (for a discussion of factors influencing academic behaviour, see Macfarlane 2016; Nygaard 2017).

Thomas (2015) in a stimulating short paper on relevance in academic research poses an important question: since many non-academic actors also undertake policy research (e.g. consultants or in-house policy researchers working for tourist boards or NGOs), what is the 'distinctive contribution that might arise from that research being undertaken by academics'? As he points out, the answer provided, implicitly or explicitly, usually encompasses notions of independence and rigour (see also Dredge 2015). His suggestion is that as those working in universities cannot lay exclusive claim to these qualities, university academics might do well to articulate a more sophisticated explanation of their unique contribution. In spite of sustained and purposive questioning, none of those interviewed were able (or chose) to do so.

RESEARCH QUALITY, TEACHING AND IMPACT

That the research in marginal fields such as of tourism and related subjects may be of insufficient quality to act as a bedrock for impact is rarely discussed in the literature. Instead, many academic commentaries routinely repeat a somewhat imperious rhetoric that dispenses with the need for evidence. By way of illustration, Melissen and Koens (2016: 11) recently asserted that the work of a particular academic 'is a classic example of close cooperation, with both industry and academic benefits being created through that cooperation'. There is little or no evidence in their paper or the paper they cite to suggest that this is the case. This lack of critical reflection is curious given the widely acknowledged lack of impact.

Could it be that potential 'users' of academic research in tourism do not think it is sufficiently sophisticated? The findings of an ESRC funded study of knowledge acquisition among very senior managers in commercial tourism organisations suggest that this may be the case (Thomas 2012). Further, Airey et al.'s (2015) recent assessment, which was informed in part by official audits of research quality in the UK, Australia and China, also highlighted the relative weakness of tourism research *vis-a-vis* other fields and disciplines. Two experienced researchers interviewed for this book, both of whom have strong international reputations for their research and scholarship, stated the following:

> The research quality in tourism remains disappointing. There is some very good stuff, but there is a very long tail, I would argue … It's about rigour but it's also about innovation and looking at problems in a different way … I think a lot of what we do is a bit hum drum and a bit routine.

and

> Tourism, I think... you know this as well as I do... A lot of people who
> work in tourism don't get research money because they don't apply for
> it, or the application's quite poor ... and if you compared the tourism
> ones, the quality of the application with the others, very few of them got
> through to the second round. I only know one that got through to the
> second round - and then did not get funding. So it's the quality of the
> application, really, to a degree.

The very low number of peer-reviewed research council grants listed in
Table 4.7 of Chapter 4 provides a degree of corroboration to this perspective. In such circumstances, academic research in tourism is not
likely to yield impact, especially when the sector remains unconvinced
of the need to utilise academic knowledge as a means of innovating and
improving competitiveness (see Chapter 2).

Such perspectives might be juxtaposed with recent reviews of the
impact of professional education. The Chartered Association of Business
Schools' (CABS) recent review of executive education, for example, provides illustration of how longer-term research-informed development
programmes yield benefits to participants because there is time and space
to encourage development. Some of those interviewed made similar sug-
gestions. The following three comments illustrate the point clearly:

> Personally, I would rather consider, if I'd had an impact anywhere, it was
> through the teaching of research students and the building up of capac-
> ity in tourism, to show people how to do research and demonstrate their
> research as being useful. Personally, I think, for me, if there is a legacy that
> I would leave behind, it is that impact on PhD students, not on the wider
> community.

and

> ... they (practitioners) see things differently as a result of attending my
> courses. More attending my courses than reading my work, in truth... And
> a number of people say to me "I get a real sense of satisfaction of coming
> back to your course, hearing some of the same advice and being able to say
> yes, I have done that because I was here last time, and here's some of the
> things he's saying now that I haven't changed yet, and I'll go back and do
> it now." That's just such an amazing adrenaline (sic).

and

> If I am honest, even though I use the discourse of impact, the only real effect I have, if I have one at all, is with the students I spend most time with.

As any experienced academic tutor knows, intellectual development takes time and, within universities, is most effective when well organised and structured. Parsons and Thomas (2015) draw attention to a case study that exemplifies—from a non-marginal field—the effectiveness of combining high-quality research with structured teaching or other development activity, to achieve non-academic impact. In the case they cite, researchers secured substantial research council grant funding to learn how companies grew and, separately, how they learned. They combined the two to develop a programme that resulted in evident (verified) changes in practice. While that level of comprehensiveness is probably a very distant prospect for university tourism departments, the potential of achieving impact by offering a high-quality education to students is not.

Suggesting the achievement of impact via the education of students is hardly new or radical (see from Boyer 1990 to Hinton-Smith 2012). Others have made similar connections in the context of tourism (for recent examples, see Ting and Cheng 2017; Carnicelli and Boluk 2017) and have made a compelling case for the potentially valuable influence of research-informed teaching in this field (e.g. Lugosi et al. 2009; Thomas and Harris 2001). One of the consequences of the prominence given to various measures of productivity in performance-based funding systems such as REF is often a distancing of teaching from research (Visser-Wijnveen et al. 2010). If this is the case in tourism studies, there are dangers of undermining the quality of education offered to students on the false promise that they will have access to tutors who are leading researchers (because they are working elsewhere and pursuing other constituencies).

Conclusion

This chapter has shown that academic researchers working in the marginal fields of tourism and related subjects generally welcome the impact agenda. Arguably, their relative powerlessness as a group of disorganised workers also encourages compliance with broader neoliberal higher education policies, leading to an emphasis on performativity in the face of systematic state power. To that extent, they are no different from many others in various fields and disciplines.

The academics interviewed tend to explain (away) their lack of impact as a deficiency on the part of practitioners (including tourism policy-makers) or as dysfunctional communication. Those that lay claim to research that contributes to social and environmental improvement and perceive themselves to be successful in effecting change are often most critical of the disposition of others. Yet, their analysis of the dynamics of impact reveals little or no appreciation of related ontological and epistemological debates (e.g. Van de Ven 2007); instead, there is a reliance of homespun worldliness. None of those who declared themselves critical social scientists embedded sophisticated anti-, critical or progressive performative approaches in their stances on impact. In these circumstances, it is unlikely that changes to behaviour will emerge, leading to more research impact.

Informed by documentary sources such as feedback on REF and the testimony of influential researchers, the chapter also questioned the quality of tourism research. The prospect of only incremental improvement in quality and the limited availability of 'credible' research (in the eyes of non-academics) inevitably acts as a limiting factor for research impact.

The aspiration to engage in research-informed teaching did not feature prominently during the interviews with academic researchers. Nevertheless, several participants articulated the idea that their greatest impact is achieved via the education of students. A reorientation of work towards this activity might—somewhat ironically perhaps—increase research impact as students enter the labour market and participate more ably in society.

References

Airey, D., Tribe, J., & Benckendorff, P. (2015). The managerial gaze: The long tail of tourism education and research. *Journal of Travel Research, 54*(2), 139–151.

Ball, S. J. (2012). Performativity, commodification and commitment: An I-spy guide to the neoliberal university. *British Journal of Educational Studies, 60*(1), 17–28.

Bartunek, J. M., & Rynes, S. L. (2014). Academics and practitioners are alike and unlike: The paradoxes of academic-practitioner relationships. *Journal of Management, 40*(5), 1181–1201.

Boyer, E. L. (1990). *Scholarship reconsidered: Priorities of the professoriate*. San Francisco: Jossey-Bass.

Carnicelli, S., & Boluk, K. (2017). The promotion of social justice: Service learning for transformative education. *Journal of Hospitality, Leisure, Sport & Tourism Education, 21*(B): 126–134.

Chartered Association of Business Schools (CABS). (2017). *The impact of executive education*. London: CABS.

Clarke, C. A., & Knights, D. (2015). Careering through academia: Securing identities or engaging ethical subjectivities? *Human Relations, 68*(12), 1865–1888.

Dredge, D. (2015). Does relevance matter in academic policy research? *Journal of Policy Research in Tourism, Leiure and Events, 7*(2), 173–177.

Fournier, V., & Grey, C. (2000). At the critical moment: Conditions and prospects for critical management studies. *Human Relations, 53*(1), 7–32.

Gond, J.-P., Cabantous, L., Harding, N., & Learmonth, M. (2016). What do we mean by performativity in organizational and management theory? The uses and abuses of performativity. *International Journal of Management Reviews, 18*, 440–463.

Hinton-Smith, T. (Ed.). (2012). *Widening participation in higher education: Casting the net wide?* Basingstoke: Palgrave Macmillan.

Knights, D., & Clarke, C. A. (2014). It's a bittersweet symphony, this life: Academic selves and insecure identities at work. *Organization Studies, 35*(3), 335–357.

Kyvik, S. (2013). The academic researcher role: Enhancing the expectations and improved performance. *Higher Education, 65*, 525–538.

Lugosi, P., Lynch, P., & Morrison, A. (2009). Critical hospitality management research. *The Service Industries Journal, 29*(10), 1465–1478.

Macfarlane, B. (2016). From identity to identities: A story of fragmentation. *Higher Education Research & Development, 35*(5), 1083–1085.

Melissen, F., & Koens, K. (2016). Adding researchers' behaviour to the research agenda: Bridging the science-policy gap in sustainable tourism mobility. *Journal of Sustainable Tourism, 24*(3), 335–349.

Nygaard, L. P. (2017). Publishing and perishing: An academic literacies framework for investigating research productivity. *Studies in Higher Education, 42*(3), 519–532.

Page, D. (2017). Conspicuous practice: Self-surveillance and commodification in English education. *International Studies in Sociology of Education*. https://doi.org/10.1080/09620214.2017.1351309.

Parsons, D., & Thomas, R. (2015). *Evaluating the economic impact of social science*. Swindon: Economic and Social Research Council. http://www.esrc.ac.uk/files/research/research-and-impact-evaluation/lbu-valuation-study/.

Ruegg, W. (Ed.). (2004). *A history of the university in Europe: Volume III universities in the nineteenth and early twentieth centuries (1800–1945)*. Cambridge: Cambridge University Press.

Ryan, S. (2012). Academic zombies. A failure of resistance or a means of survival? *Australian Universities Review, 54*(2), 3–11.

Slee, P. R. H. (1986). *Learning and a liberal education: The study of modern history in the universities of Oxford, Cambridge and Manchester 1800–1914*. Manchester: Manchester University Press.

Smyth, J. (2017). *The toxic university: Zombie leadership, academic rock stars, and neoliberal ideology*. London: Palgrave Macmillan.

Spicer, A., Alvesson, M., & Karreman, D. (2009). Critical performativity: The unfinished business of critical management studies. *Human Relations, 62,* 537–560.

Spicer, A., Alvesson, M., & Karreman, D. (2016). Extending critical performativity. *Human Relations, 69*(2), 225–249.

Thomas, H. (2005). Pressures, purpose and collegiality in UK planning education. *Planning Theory and Practice, 6*(2), 238–247.

Thomas, H. (2010). Knowing the city: Local coalitions, knowledge and research. In C. Allen & R. Imrie (Eds.), *The knowledge business* (pp. 77–92). Farnham: Ashgate.

Thomas, H. (2015). Does relevance matter in academic policy research? A comment on Dredge. *Journal of Policy research in Tourism, Leisure and Events, 7*(2), 178–182.

Thomas, R. (2011). Academics as policy-makers: (Not) Researching tourism and events policy from the inside. *Current Issues in Tourism, 14*(6), 493–506.

Thomas, R. (2012). Business elites, universities and knowledge transfer in tourism. *Tourism Management, 33*(3), 553–561.

Thomas, R. (2017a). *New spaces in cultural tourism: Universities and innovation*. Keynote presentation to the New spaces in cultural tourism conference. University of Novi Sad, Serbia, September.

Thomas, R. (2017b). *Making sense of our business engagement: Illusions, aspirations and achievements*. Keynote presentation to the 4th International Conference on Events, University of Central Florida, USA, December.

Thomas, R., & Harris, V. (2001). Exploring connections between teaching and research in hospitality management. *International Journal of Hospitality Management, 20*(3), 245–257.

Thomas, R., & Ormerod, N. (2017). The (almost) imperceptible impact of tourism research on policy and practice. *Tourism Management, 62,* 379–389.

Thomas, R., Shaw, G., & Page, S. J. (2011). Understanding small firms in tourism: A perspective on research trends and challenges. *Tourism Management, 32*(5), 963–976.

Ting, D. H., & Cheng, C. F. C. (2017). Measuring the marginal effect of pro-environmental behaviour: Guided learning and behavioural enhancement. *Journal of Hospitality, Leisure, Sport & Tourism Education, 20*, 16–26.

Van de Ven, A. H. (2007). *Engaged scholarship: A guide for organisational and social research.* Oxford: Oxford University Press.

Visser-Wijnveen, G. J., Van Driel, J. H., Van der Rijst, R. M., Verloop, N., & Visser, A. (2010). The ideal research-teaching nexus in the eyes of academics: Building profiles. *Higher Education Research & Development, 29*(2), 195–210.

Watermeyer, R. (2016). Impact in the REF: Issues and obstacles. *Studies on Higher Education, 41*(2), 199–214.

Watts, R. (2017). *Public universities, managerialism and the value of higher education.* London: Palgrave Macmillan.

Wickert, C., & Schaefer, S. M. (2015). Towards a progressive understanding of performativity in critical management studies. *Human Relations, 68*(1), 107–130.

CHAPTER 6

Conclusion: A Return to Education

... if I'd had an impact anywhere, it was through the teaching of research
students and the building up of capacity in tourism ...
Research professor interviewed for this book

Abstract Calls by research policy-makers for greater non-academic impact will not yield the intended outcomes in marginal fields such as tourism. This is because practitioner (and organisational) behaviours are contrary to official conceptualisations and because of the orientation of researchers and the quality of their work. This concluding chapter advocates a new social contract that emphasises the role of educating students as a means of creating knowledge flows from universities. Research with impact might then be achievable. For policy-makers, this would mean enabling university departments to educate effectively rather than encouraging them to generate 'noise' and, in most cases, to make exaggerated claims of impact.

Keywords Tourism studies · Impact · Research assessment

UK governments have utilised some form of performance-based university research funding system since the mid-1980s. Developed as part of

© The Author(s) 2018
R. Thomas, *Questioning the Assessment of Research
Impact*, Palgrave Critical University Studies,
https://doi.org/10.1007/978-3-319-95723-4_6

a wider set of market-oriented interventions, its consistently stated purpose has been to differentiate institutions based on official notions of research quality and productivity. This has precipitated the emergence of a neoliberal managerial discourse and inspired the evolution of strategies (and game playing) associated with enabling institutions to 'perform'. 'Success' results in enhanced institutional status (usually a ranking) and additional discretionary funding. This is broadly consistent with research policy developments in many other parts of the world (OECD 2014; Stern 2016). The Research Excellence Framework (REF), the system currently operating in the UK, makes no distinction, in principle, between disciplines or fields of study.

Since the inclusion of impact in 2014 and its increasing prominence for the 2021 exercise, the claim has been made that REF bolsters engagement with non-academic constituencies; this is seen as advantageous to the economy and society (Stern 2016). Few would question the existence of symbiotic relationships between universities and the private or public sectors and their implications for innovation in some, notably knowledge intensive, sectors. *The Times Higher Education*, a weekly magazine, recently reported rankings of universities in the Nature Index Innovation (17–23 August, 2017: 12). As it states, 'the list measures the influence an institution's research has had on innovation by calculating the citations of research articles in patents owned by third parties, rather than those owned by institutions themselves'. The argument presented in this book does not extend to these contexts. The contribution (impact) universities make to innovation in tourism, now and in the foreseeable future, has, however, been contested.

There is an established body of research suggesting that academic research in tourism has little impact on non-academic constituencies (e.g. Ryan 2001; Ritchie and Ritchie 2002; Ruhanen 2008; Thomas 2012; Thomas and Ormerod 2017). Yet, commentators often appear to accept as axiomatic the value of academic research to practitioners. The tone of the following illustrates the point:

The results herein strongly suggest that relatively little knowledge transfer … is taking place between the knowledge generators in the academic community on one side, and managers and operators in the private and public sectors responsible for tourism and hospitality development on the other. (Frechtling 2004: 107)

... insights developed in academia have not always resulted in progress in practice. (Melissen and Koens 2016: 336)

Accordingly, universities are generators of knowledge and other actors seen as recipients. The consistent challenge becomes conceptualised primarily as one of communication and engagement. There is little questioning (publicly) of research quality and relevance to practitioners. This book has suggested that while there are instances of both high-quality research and of impact, the majority of research undertaken in tourism and related fields offers little novel insight that is of relevance to practitioners and is not, therefore, likely to yield impact. Moreover, there are no convincing reasons to suppose that this will change in the short or medium term, if at all. Thus, an increased emphasis on impact becomes distracting and diverts attention from more valuable academic activity.

In making this case, the starting point was to consider the literature on innovation in tourism and related sectors, paying particular attention to the role of external knowledge in the innovation process. Influential conceptualisations were explored and a wide range of empirical evidence evaluated. It was noted that universities do not feature prominently in most accounts of how innovations occur in tourism or in how tourism policy evolves. Attention then moved to professional associations, which are often treated as valuable mediators for knowledge exchange between practitioners and universities. Contrary to orthodox accounts, the analysis suggests that collaborative activity between professional associations in tourism and universities represents little more than a benign harnessing of academic work to create stories for their members; academic research does not inform its policy or practices, or those of its members.

Several additional arguments are presented to help explain the almost imperceptible impact of tourism researchers. The first, briefly, involved rejecting the explanatory value of commonly trumpeted forms of market failure and recognising that universities, tourism businesses and tourism policy-makers operate within marginal and largely separate (but well defined) communities of practice. This observation has significant (ontological and epistemological) implications for how the process of knowledge construction is (re)conceptualised by various constituencies. Secondly, the quality of tourism research, and its potential to influence policy and practice, has been questioned. It is often the case that where academics do lay claim to impact, it is based on relatively routine consultancy work that others may undertake equally effectively rather than anything peculiarly associated with universities. Thirdly, regardless of research orientations that often emphasise the economically liberating role of tourism, or its contribution to intercultural understanding and social improvement, there was little evidence of progressive or critical performativity; there were rare instances of academics setting out to support the powerless but little sense of academics engaging in 'acts of resistance' or plans for subversion.

An important casualty of the growing focus on impact is the reduced emphasis given to the teaching of students. Some universities, internationally, approach the challenge of impact differently and focus on research-informed teaching, and seeing the tutelage of students as the greatest area of impact. A brief discussion of two approaches illustrates the potential of alternative approaches to what is currently practised in the UK. This should not be seen as an endorsement of either or both; it is designed to do no more than help prompt a reconsideration of how academics in tourism and related fields might adopt a more meaningful approach to the impact agenda.

The School of Hotel and Tourism Management (SHTM) at Hong Kong Polytechnic University has a strong reputation for the research outputs of its staff and for the quality of the educational experience it offers its students (Park et al. 2011; Severt et al. 2009). For the purposes of this chapter, however, what is most interesting about the School is its creation and management of a highly successful hotel, namely Hotel ICON. It has 262 guest rooms, 77 club rooms and 26 suites. The hotel is used for research purposes as well as to train students. Yet, unlike many training establishments, it is commercially viable and is among the most highly regarded hotels in Hong Kong. Indeed, at the time of writing (May 2018), it was rated 3rd from 727 hotels in Hong Kong by Trip Advisor based on almost 7000 reviews (https://www.tripadvisor.co.uk/Hotel_Review-g294217-d2031570-Reviews-Hotel_ICON-Hong_Kong.html) and was listed by Trip Advisor as one of the best 25 hotels in China. It has also won awards for innovation from the United Nations World Tourism Organisation (UNWTO) (Chon 2014).

A visit to the hotel's website (http://www.hotel-icon.com/#/our-story) reveals it to be somewhat typical of good quality accommodation providers. One of the few indications that this is a different kind of enterprise is tucked away in the 'about' section where it states:

Hotel ICON is a very special hotel with an equally special purpose. Not only does it embody all the creative energy and spirit of Hong Kong, it's a learning environment on which the aspirations of future hoteliers come to life as part of the Hong Kong Polytechnic University and an extension of its School of Hotel and Tourism Management (SHTM). In our little universe, students, teachers and seasoned hospitality professionals come together united by one goal: to make your stay utterly memorable and pleasurable. (http://www.hotel-icon.com/about-the-hotel.aspx#/unlike-any-other)

Chon (2014) provides a very readable account of the antecedents of Hotel ICON and its central role as a place for education and research. By his account, the research that is most valued is that which can be used to enhance industrial management practices. Three guestrooms have been set aside, for example, to explore design issues and their implications for operations and the guest experience. They are used to test products developed with suppliers, and the results are made available to the hotel sector more generally or written about in journals. Impact is also claimed via the delivery of executive education programmes.

One area of the building where knowledge exchange is perhaps most consciously promoted is called the 'Crossroads'. It is intended to be a place where academic staff, students and practitioners are able to meet to share ideas and knowledge. Its significance as an aspiration is demonstrated by the declaration on the wall which states that:

Many educators and industry leaders from around the world cross their paths here at The Crossroads... The Crossroads is where ideas are shared, views exchanged and knowledge passed on from generation to generation. (Chon 2014: 44)

Chon's (2014) discussion of the approach and practices of SHTM suggest that the greatest emphasis is on providing students with an exceptionally high-quality education that is unambiguously linked to academic research and professional practice.

The Rosen College of Hospitality Management (RCHM) at the University of Central Florida (UCF) displays similarities with HKPU. It is regarded as a leading teaching and research centre (Park et al. 2011; Severt et al. 2009) which boasts long-term mutually beneficial relationships with practitioners. Pizam et al. (2013) provide a succinct historical account of the development of RCHM and its orientation. They also note that its mission is to 'develop future generations of global hospitality and tourism leaders representing all industry segments in the hospitality capital of the world, through innovative academic programs, cutting-edge research and strong industry and community partnerships' (Pizam et al. 2013: 247–248). Again, what is emphasised is that research informs teaching and that those who have been taught are able to gain good jobs and feel well equipped to succeed.

These two cases illustrate that even among those university tourism departments that are regarded as being closely aligned with industry, their most prominent claims to impact come—unashamedly—from undertaking research and using it to inform the education of students. With reason, many readers of a book that sits within Palgrave's *Critical University Studies* series will take issue with this. Most academics working within British tourism departments, however, currently offer few alternative visions. They choose instead to subscribe to dominant discourses and to make somewhat delusional claims to impact. Even those that espouse critical (tourism) scholarship ignore ideas of anti- or critical performativity and adopt a narrow framing of impact. Reconnecting (critical) research with teaching offers those keen to demonstrate their impact a much more fruitful set of possibilities to explore. That way, academics operating at the margins, or those who may feel marginalised, might make a distinctive social, cultural or economic contribution (impact) via the education of their students.

REFERENCES

Chon, K. (2014). *Leading the way: The story of STHM and Hotel ICON*. Hong Kong: HKPU.

Frechtling, D. C. (2004). Assessment of tourism/hospitality journals' role in knowledge transfer: An exploratory study. *Journal of Travel Research, 43,* 100–107.

Melissen, F., & Koens, K. (2016). Adding researchers' behaviour to the research agenda: Bridging the science-policy gap in sustainable tourism mobility. *Journal of Sustainable Tourism, 24*(3): 335–349.

Organisation for Economic Cooperation and Development (OECD). (2014). *OECD Science, Technology and Industry Outlook 2014.* Paris: OECD.

Park, K., Phillips, W. J., Canter, D. D., & Abbot, J. (2011). Hospitality and tourism research rankings by author, university, and country using six major journals: The first decade of the new millennium. *Journal of Hospitality & Tourism Research, 35*(3), 381–416.

Pizam, A., Okumus, F., & Hutchinson, J. (2013). Forming a long-term industry-university partnership: The case of Rosen College of Hospitality Management. *Worldwide Hospitality and Tourism Themes, 5*(3), 244–254.

Ritchie, R. J. B., & Ritchie, J. R. B. (2002). A framework for an industry supported destination marketing information system. *Tourism Management, 23,* 439–454.

Ruhanen, L. (2008). Progressing the sustainability debate: A knowledge management approach to sustainable tourism planning. *Current Issues in Tourism, 11*(5), 429–455.

Ryan, C. (2001). Academia-industry tourism research links: States of confusion. *Pacific Tourism Review, 5*(3 & 4), 83–95.

Severt, D. E., Tesone, D. V., Bottorff, T. J., & Carpenter, M. L. (2009). A world ranking of the top 100 hospitality and tourism programs. *Journal of Hospitality & Tourism Research, 33*(4), 451–470.

Stern, L. N. (2016). *Building on success and learning from experience: An independent review of the Research Excellence Framework.* London: Department for Business, Energy and Industrial Strategy.

Thomas, R. (2012). Business elites, universities and knowledge transfer in tourism. *Tourism Management, 33*(3), 553–561.

Thomas, R., & Ormerod, N. (2017). The (almost) imperceptible impact of tourism research on policy and practice. *Tourism Management, 62,* 379–389.

INDEX

© The Editor(s) (if applicable) and The Author(s) 2018   131
R. Thomas, *Questioning the Assessment of Research
Impact*, Palgrave Critical University Studies,
https://doi.org/10.1007/978-3-319-95723-4

Printed by Printforce, the Netherlands